The Dark Side of International Tax Law

Giuseppe Marino

The Dark Side of International Tax Law

Pecunia non olet

G. Giappichelli Editore

Springer

Giuseppe Marino
Faculty of Law
University of Milan
Milan, Italy

ISBN 978-3-032-08158-2 ISBN 978-3-032-08159-9 (eBook)
https://doi.org/10.1007/978-3-032-08159-9

This Springer imprint is published by the registered company Springer Nature Switzerland AG
The registered company address is: Gewerbestrasse 11, 6330 Cham, Switzerland

To my beloved Family whose value goes far beyond the pecunia *of all the world*

Competing Interests The author has no competing interests to declare that are relevant to the content of this manuscript.

Contents

Chapter 1
Preamble

Contents

Taxes are the price we pay for a civilized society (Oliver Wendell Holmes Jr, US Supreme Court Justice), and law is the last step involved in the evolution of taxation. At the beginning, indeed, it is fair to recognize that philosophy, politics and economics (PPE) are involved in sequence in the discussion of public finances, together with history, which is the glue connecting these human sciences. Technology is also playing a more dramatic role in the development of taxation than ever before, and it should now have the same academic dignity as PPE. Priorities should always be clear. In practice, you never know what comes first among PPE or technology, and once tax law enters into force, it is rather easier to change it for the worse than for the best, since societies always request more public goods, and when public finances are not enough, public debt dangerously enters in the game. Sometimes, case law straightens its defects, although history shows that only wars, revolutions and scandals bring progress in tax law matters. This is the reason why the law here becomes only one of the perspectives of taxation.

The same holds true for international taxation, that is, when a sovereign State asks for money from its own taxpayers on their worldwide ability to pay, as well as from foreign taxpayers on their ability to pay that is located inside its own territory. Once PPE discussions on the indices of ability to pay are set (catching wealth, income and/or consumption), the framework of international tax law appears.

Unfortunately, the international tax rules of a State might overlap with the set of rules adopted by other States where either the above ability to pay or the taxpayers are located, resulting in double taxation. This is the reason why international tax law is a two-faced Janus: on the one hand, domestic tax law is involved, while on the other hand, international law, both treaty-based and customary, comes on stage.

G. Marino, *The Dark Side of International Tax Law*,
https://doi.org/10.1007/978-3-032-08159-9_1

Maybe it could be better to refer to Dr Jekyll and Mr Hyde since the international community generally plays for good, while single States play for evil.

Another complication must be added to the above international tax chess, and that is whenever a State, more or less powerful and more or less consciously, has its tax system or a specific tax regime that is honey for foreign taxpayers who want to buy it for their ability to pay inducing comparison, attraction, and competition, so creating double non-taxation that brings financial damage to the States to which the taxpayers belong. This is the "pecunia non olet" perspective, or the offshore shadow, that is old like human beings, happens more than often, and belongs to all countries, as the financial scandals demonstrate.

The scope of this booklet is to help understand the principles of international tax law and to look behind their dark side in order to interpret the dynamics that drive States in the exercise of their taxing (as well as non-taxing) power within the international condominium. There is no space in this booklet to discuss solidarity, in all its declinations, and taxation, which is left within the philosophy of domestic taxation, where instances of the social community prevail over those of single individuals. On the side of international taxpayers, indeed, there is neither a legal nor a moral obligation to pay taxes elsewhere, only a factual obligation to do it somewhere.

I wish the reader could approach the effort by listening to the album *The Dark Side of the Moon*, registered by Pink Floyd at the Abbey Road Studios in London and played all over the world as of 1973, with particular reference to the song *Money*, since that is indeed the matter we shall be talking about: "Money, it's a crime, share it fairly but don't take a slice of my pie".

International tax is a great example of how law is a matter of perspective. Depending on whether the driver is the international condominium, a part of it (i.e. the European floor), or a single State, the financial interests and the related solutions to take care of may change like the skin of a chameleon. In other words, the coherence of the international tax regime embodied in the bilateral and multilateral tax treaties may not be the coherence of the international tax regime embodied at the domestic level. In between, it is worth noting that there might be the European level, where Member States always try to distinguish their position and gain on it, and if they fail to, it is only because they believe in a superior hierarchical reaction.

Global ambitions and local hypocrisies reshuffle the game of international tax in such a way that it is difficult to identify winners and losers other than those in the long run. There might even be an international tax regime in principle, but in practice, States care only so far as it is convenient to share it. The single tax principle of wealth, income and consumption is never an assumption, only a trend where one taxation is too little and double taxation is too much since, as Tacitus (56–120 B.C.) already wrote in the "Annales" (13, 50), "Boni Pastoris est tondere pecus, non deglubere" (the sheep must be sheared, not killed). By the way, *pecus* is the root for *pecunia,* as in the ancient world, sheep have always been sacrificed to obtain the grace of God.

Furthermore, taxation and international taxation are part of public finance that is strictly connected to the management of economic powers that are driven by philosophy and politics. In this context, the legal framework generally follows, and the State that has been showing economic supremacy at the international level since the nineteenth century is certainly the United States, for good and evil. Depending on the PPE interpretation, the US government has been giving *pro tempore* to its worldwide public finance interests; international taxation has been embodied in US law and, consequently, has been circulating within the international community. Reuven Avi-Yonah has periodized the history of US international taxation system into: (i) the age of benefits (1918–1960) through the definition of "economic allegiance" which is used to justify both source-based taxation and residence-based taxation; (ii) the age of neutrality (1961–1980) that left back the emphasis on benefits and fairness in light of efficiency, which in the international context was translated into neutrality; (iii) the age of competition (1981–1997) when, in an increasing globalization, the competitiveness of US multinationals in face of increasing foreign competition was as crucial as the need to attract increasingly mobile foreign capital; and, last but not least, (iv) the age of an alleged tax cooperation (from 1998) that is marked by a different response to globalization than unilateral competition, acting in concert with major trading partners to reduce both double taxation and double non taxation.

The Trump Administration's slogan "America First" is marking a new trend in the US international tax policy, with the *Tax Cuts and Jobs Act* of 2017 being a protectionist tax reshoring that is overriding tax cooperation, and the new slogan "Make America Great Again" of his second mandate seems no different. A new international tax (dis)order is appearing on stage, envisaging the birth of another age within the US international taxation, or, better, the return to the scopes pursued in earlier ages. History repeats itself.

It is not imaginable to study international tax law without an analysis of how US tax law embodies the underlying norms of the regime, since the rest of the world, including offshore countries, has always been a follower.

If the world is a follower, the role of Italy within the international tax chess is that of Cinderella, only recently resulting in a charming international tax system like other small countries successfully did, sad but true. Nevertheless, Italy is a beautiful country, and this is the reason why the attitude is one of indulgence and much love in the analysis of its perspective.

After philosophy, politics and economics of international taxation and its related history, the investigation enters into the following steps: 1) *who* has the right to exercise the power to tax, namely the jurisdiction to tax; 2) *what* to tax among active and passive income; 3) *how* to exercise the power to tax, through tax returns or withholding tax; 4) *how much* to tax through transfer pricing methodology; 5) international taxation as international law; 6) principles of European tax law; 7) tax treaties; 8) Base Erosion Profit Shifting (BEPS 1.0) and BEPS 2.0; 9) some selected hottest topics with the latest international tax recommendations of the Organisation for Economic Co-operation and Development (OECD) as well as the last American tax whims.

One final consideration. International taxation and international tax law have nothing to do today with tariffs and duties on international trade that are measures protecting domestic markets. In a globalized world, there should be globalized markets with no tariffs or duties. However, this is not always true and leads to asymmetries and inefficiencies.

In conclusion, as the Sicilian Tancredi Falconeri reminds his uncle Don Fabrizio Corbera, Prince of Salina, in the masterpiece novel "The Leopard" written by Giuseppe Tomasi di Lampedusa, everything must change because everything remains as it is, and the opinion is that only by exploring the perennial reshuffles behind the stage of international taxation could the reader understand how this important piece of social science really works. A special and warm thank must be addressed to two Leopards of international tax law, Jacques Malherbe, Professor of law emeritus of the Catholic University of Louvain, and Reuven Avi-Yonah, Irwin I. Cohn Professor of law at the University of Michigan, who friendly and irresponsibly supported my ambition for this publication.

Reference

di Lampedusa GT (1991) The Leopard, Everyman edition

Chapter 2
Philosophy of International Taxation

Contents

2.1 Introduction

In the ancient world, taxation was not discussed in the technical or institutional sense that we acknowledge today. However, philosophers like Aristotle and Cicero laid down philosophical foundations for later conceptions of fair taxation rooted in their broader reflections on justice, the state, and civic responsibility.

In "Politics" and "Nicomachean Ethics" (350–322 B.C.), Aristotle presents a vision of the polis (city-state) as a community aimed at achieving the highest human good—*eudaimonia*, or flourishing. Within this framework, taxation can be understood as part of the duties citizens have toward supporting public goods. Aristotle makes a key distinction between distributive justice, which allocates resources according to merit or contribution, and corrective justice, which rectifies inequalities. Applied to taxation, this suggests a proportional system in which individuals contribute based on their capacity. Importantly, he stresses the need for a balanced society—extremes of wealth and poverty undermine political stability and justice. Thus, while not advocating explicit redistribution, Aristotle's political philosophy supports the idea that wealthier citizens may bear spontaneously a greater fiscal responsibility for the health of the State (the so-called *Leitourgìa*).

G. Marino, *The Dark Side of International Tax Law*,
https://doi.org/10.1007/978-3-032-08159-9_2

On the other hand, Cicero, writing in the context of the Roman Empire, offers a more legally oriented view in works like "De Re Publica" (54–51, B.C.), "De Legibus" (52–42, B.C.), and "De Officiis" (44 B.C.). He emphasizes natural law, arguing that justice and the legitimacy of any law—including taxation—must be based on reason and the universal principles of right. For Cicero, taxation is legitimate only when it aligns with the justice, moderation, and consent of the government. He defends the sanctity of private property but acknowledges that the State may impose taxes if they are fair and serve the public interest. Excessive or arbitrary taxation, in contrast, is a mark of tyranny and should be resisted. Statesmen, according to Cicero, have a moral duty to govern for the benefit of all citizens, not for private gain.

In conclusion, while neither Aristotle nor Cicero offered a systematic theory of taxation, their reflections provide enduring insights. Both philosophers view taxation as an extension of justice and civic duty—not merely an economic necessity but a moral and political instrument. Taxes must be proportional, fair, and oriented toward public goods, always respecting the delicate balance between individual rights and collective responsibility.

While taxation continued in practice during the Middle Ages (especially by the Church and monarchies), discussions were often framed in theological or feudal terms, rather than philosophical ones like tax fairness, equity and the role of the State.

2.2 Taxation During the Enlightenment Period

Only during the Age of Enlightenment in Europe did philosophy regain its status as the language to approach human sciences like politics, economics and ultimately, law. Taxation is no exception.

Naples contributed to the Enlightenment with many scholars with a philosophical background whose ideas anticipated modern debates on tax justice, economic incentives and state intervention in fiscal policy. The flagship is with Giambattista Vico (1668–1744), who wrote "La Scienza nuova" (*The New Science*) (1725), where he describes that taxation evolves with history and unfair taxation leads to decline; then Carlo Antonio Broggia (1698–1767), merchant and economist, who wrote "Trattato de' tributi, delle monete, e del governo politico della sanità" (*Treaty of taxes, of currencies, and of political government of health*) (1743), supporting that taxes should be proportionate and used for public services. Aiming to promote prosperity through business and commerce, Broggia advises the taxation of inherited wealth at a greater rate than wealth accruing through commerce. Though both direct and indirect taxation are recommended, the former should not be levied on earned income. He also argued about simplified customs procedures and low import duties, the right to export and the dangers of monopoly. Antonio Genovesi (1713–1769) was granted the first Chair in Europe of Economics at the University of Naples in 1755 and wrote "Lezioni di economia civile" (L*essons of Civil*

Economy) (1765), where he emphasizes that taxes should encourage economic growth and education. Jurist Giacinto Dragonetti (1738–1818), who wrote "Trattato delle virtù e dei premi" (*On Virtues and Rewards*) (1766), where he states that taxation should reward virtue and productivity. Philosopher and jurist Gaetano Filangieri (1753–1788), who wrote "La scienza della legislazione" (*The Science of Legislation*) (1780), claimed that taxation should be progressive and transparent and influenced Benjamin Franklin and the writing of the United States Constitution. Abbot Ferdinando Galiani (1728–1787), who wrote "Della moneta" (*On currency*) (1780), where taxation should balance incentives, avoid inflation and adapt to economic cycles. Finally, jurist Francesco Mario Pagano (1748–1799), who was a leading figure in the Neapolitan Revolution of 1799, found death by Bourbon restoration. His "Political Essays" (1783) supports that a Republic must have a fair and transparent tax system reflecting the influence of Genovesi and Galiani, who also advocated for a tax system that promotes economic growth rather than stifling it.

Nevertheless, France has also contributed to the Enlightenment with some masterpieces on the relationship between the State and its citizens, including their economic contribution. Montesquieu (1689–1755) wrote a pillar being "De l'esprit des lois" (*The spirit of the laws*) (1748), where he explores taxation extensively, emphasizing that taxes should be proportionate and not arbitrary. He distinguishes between taxation in despotic, monarchical and republican States, arguing that in a well-governed Republic, taxes are lighter and more fairly distributed. Jean-Jacques Rousseau (1712–1778) wrote "The Social Contract" (1762), where he argues that taxation should be consented to by the people and serve the common interest rather than the privileged few. Voltaire (1694–1778) was highly critical of the French taxation system under the Ancien Régime. His satire "L'Homme aux quarante écus" (*The Man of Forty Crowns*) (1768) tells the story of a man who finds that, after paying all the requested taxes, he has only forty écus left to live on and is a critique of excessive taxation. Finally, Alexis de Tocqueville (1805–1859) examines in "De la démocratie en Amérique" *Democracy in America*) (1835) how taxation functions in democratic societies, contrasting the relatively lighter taxation in the US with the burdensome taxes of aristocratic Europe.

All four philosophers criticize unfair taxation and emphasize its political implications. Montesquieu and Tocqueville focus on the systemic effects of taxation on governance and social stability, while Voltaire and Rousseau emphasize the moral and economic injustices of unequal tax policies. Their ideas laid the groundwork for modern discussions on progressive taxation, fiscal fairness, and the role of the government in economic policy.

2.3 Taxation for Adam Smith

However, in the decades to come, there is only one scholar remembered, and that is Adam Smith (1723–1790). He was educated as a philosopher and wrote "The Wealth of Nations" (1776), often considered the first work on modern economics, where scholars could also find the DNA of modern domestic and international tax principles, as well as the influence on Adam Smith of some Neapolitan and French readings.

There is also another reason why Adam Smith prevails over all other Enlightenment scholars as far as taxation is concerned, and it has to do with his profound impact on the British Empire's economic policies, influencing trade, taxation and governance. His theories on free markets, taxation and colonial policy shaped British economic thinking well into the nineteenth and twentieth centuries.

As far as domestic taxation is concerned, Adam Smith outlines the maxims of a tax system as 1) equity and proportionality, 2) certainty, 3) convenience of payments and 4) efficiency. Furthermore, violations must be sanctioned with penalties rising in proportion to the temptation that tax law has created, contrary to all ordinary principles of justice (Book V "Of the Revenue of the Sovereign or Commonwealth", Chapter II, Part Third). The author believes that the evident justice and utility of the foregoing maxims have recommended them to the attention of all nations. All nations have endeavoured, to the best of their judgement, to render their taxes as equal as they could contrive; as certain, as convenient to the contributor, both in the time and in the mode of payment, and in proportion to the ability to pay, namely, the revenue which they brought to the prince, as little burdensome to the people. Unfortunately, the Adam Smith review of some of the principal taxes which have taken place in different ages and countries shows that the endeavours of all nations have not in this respect been equally successful.

As far as international taxation is concerned, at that time connected with foreign trade, Adam Smith focuses on treaties of commerce that exclude certain foreign goods from customs and duties to create domestic markets where the convenience of merchants and manufacturers of both the favouring and the favoured country meets the sovereigns' expectations of an annual positive balance in gold and silver (Book IV, "Of Systems of Political OEconomy", Chapter VI). The mercantile system is indeed described as a solution to enrich both people and sovereign by providing a plentiful revenue or subsistence for the people, or more properly, to enable them to provide such revenue or subsistence for themselves, and secondly, by supplying the State or commonwealth with a revenue sufficient for the public services (Introduction to Book IV, "Of Systems of Political OEconomy").

At the time of Adam Smith, taxes were based on trade as well as the transportation of goods and real property (tariffs, customs, excise and property taxes). The income tax, he theorized at the base of the ability to pay, played an exceedingly insignificant role in the Middle Ages, while its introduction between the eighteenth and nineteenth centuries was an extraordinary case of need and urgency to finance wars (E.R.A. Seligman, "The Income Tax", The Macmillan Company, 1914).

2.4 The Income Tax and the Birth of International Taxation

The first income tax was introduced in the UK in 1799. It was established by British Prime Minister William Pitt the Younger as a temporary measure to finance military expenses during the Napoleonic Wars against France. However, the success of the modern English income tax system was in 1862, with the system of stoppage at source (the actual withholding tax). In the US, a civil war income tax was requested for the period 1861–1871, although Congress first enacted the income tax on a permanent basis in 1894, then the Supreme Court declared it unconstitutional one year later, and only after the Sixteenth Amendment to the US Constitution in 1913 did President Woodrow Wilson sign the modern personal income tax into law shortly thereafter in October 1913.

In conclusion, only in the mid-nineteenth century did scholars and politicians in the UK and the US start to view taxes based on the ability of individuals represented to pay income as an appealing alternative to taxes based on trade, as well as the transportation of goods and real property, because they could be made progressive, rather than regressive, imposing a heavier proportional burden on the rich rather than on the poor. Indirect taxes, such as on trade or consumption, are meant regressive since poor people suffer the more to survive while rich people consume and but regardless of the tax incidence. Income taxes of the modern era were designed in the UK and the US during the nineteenth century, while for the United States, the system for taxing international income is largely a creature of the period 1918–1928, a time when the income tax was still in its infancy. Rich people started to suffer as they never did in human history, although, as will be seen, the poorest always stayed in front. In other words, everyone cries feeling better.

The extension of the ability to pay collection from real taxes based on goods and properties to personal taxes based on income created a lot of problems, the solutions of which are at the base of the modern international tax system. In fact, when taxes are based on goods and properties, there is no discussion that the power to impose them stands with the State where goods and properties are located, regardless of where their owners are. However, when the taxable base is no longer an asset itself but, rather, the income that an individual can produce, by definition, from any source of labour and capital derived everywhere in the world, another player is entering into the game, and that is the State where that individual producing, possessing or disposing of that income is located.

All taxes are ultimately borne by individuals, as is the requirement for fairness, since Adam Smith is fundamentally regarded as a requirement of fairness among individuals. However, the rationale must be complicated by one more taxpayer, that is, the corporation and the separate corporate income tax, going back to the nineteenth century, both in the UK and the US.

To make a long story short, the matrix is from real taxes to personal taxes, from territorial taxation to worldwide taxation, and vice versa. It is indeed clear that most of the countries belonging to the international community adopt tax systems combining both real and personal, territorial and worldwide aspects.

As a matter of fact, the philosophical justification of international income taxation involves the following issues: 1) equity versus discrimination; 2) residence versus situs of origin; 3) passive income versus active income; 4) double taxation versus double non-taxation; 5) benefit taxation versus redistributive taxation; 6) tax competition versus tax cooperation. There is no clear justice in international taxation, only a pro tempore dominance of one edge over another.

The same issues hold true for international wealth taxation, although that collection has been ancillary until very recently, when economists of the new generation like Thomas Piketty demonstrated that the Western world now has more capital than income, and a shift back to wealth taxation at the international level is needed.

2.5 The Philosophical Pillars of International Taxation

Equity is the sole principle to justify worldwide taxation. Assume having two individual taxpayers, A and B, both located in State X, where taxpayer A only has income from any use of labour and capital within the territory of State X, and taxpayer B only has income from any source of labour and capital derived outside the territory of State X. If territorial income taxation were applied, then taxpayer A would contribute to the public expenses also for the benefit of taxpayer B, who would neither pay income tax nor contribute to public expenses of State X. To that extent, it must be accepted that only a worldwide system provides a framework for treating similarly situated individuals similarly, a concept known as horizontal equity.

A worldwide tax system helps promote the policy of income tax or wealth tax on individuals earning higher levels of income at progressively higher marginal rates, based on the theory that their greater ability to pay renders it fair to require them to shoulder a sacrifice to contribute to public expenses that is proportional to that of individuals earning a lower level of income. Thus, worldwide taxation helps to promote vertical equity.

Discrimination is the dark side of equity. Assume having two individual taxpayers, A and B, where A is in State X and B is in State Y. Both taxpayers only have income from any source of labour and capital derived within the territory of State X. However, if taxpayer B were taxed on his income with a burden heavier than that of taxpayer A, it is understood that a different and unjustified tax treatment would occur for taxpayers having the same ability to pay in the same territory.

Furthermore, equity in international taxation has an aspect other than the above-described inter-individual equity, that is, inter-nation equity, in which considerations are exploited to determine the proper division of the tax base among countries where income is produced or wealth is located, which may lead to international discrimination.

5.1. Second, *jurisdiction to tax*, being the nexus for taxation, may be defined either by the principle of residence or by that of location or origin. Taking the field of taxation, the reason why tax authorities waver between these two principles is that each may be considered as part of the still broader principle of economic interest or "economic allegiance", as against the original doctrine of "political allegiance" based on citizenship or nationality.

Part of the total amount paid according to the ability of a person to reach competing authorities, according to their economic interests under each authority. The ideal solution is that the individual's entire faculty should be taxed, but that it should be taxed only once, and that the liability should be divided among the tax territories according to their relative interests. The individual has certain economic interests in the place of his permanent residence or domicile, as well as in the place or places where his property is situated or from which his income is derived. If he makes money in one place, he generally spends it in another.

In an attempt to discover the true meaning of economic allegiance, it is clear that there are three fundamental considerations: 1) the production of wealth, when it can be assumed that tangible or intangible production has reached a complete economic destination; 2) the possession of wealth, being the time between the production of wealth and its consumption; and 3) the disposition of wealth, that is, the stage when wealth has reached its final owner, who is entitled to use it in whatever way he chooses.

There might be cases in which the "political allegiance" overlaps with the "economic allegiance", thus creating an overtaxed jurisdiction. If a State imposes an income tax on an individual on the basis of citizenship (as is the case in the United States) and another State imposes an income tax on the basis of residence, then there might be double taxation, regardless of where the income is produced, possessed or consumed. Nevertheless, there might be cases in which the "economic allegiance" overlaps with the "economic allegiance", being when at the same time two States consider an individual as being resident in their territory, and this also leads to double taxation.

The *disappearing taxpayer* is the dark side of the jurisdiction to tax and has to do with the technological revolution behind the globalization and digitalization of the world economy. In recent decades, multinational enterprises, especially Americans, have shifted their operations from one part of the world to another, making it ever easier for people to flee countries where taxes are high or to avoid taxes altogether by doing business in cyberspace. It is both a matter of sovereignty as well as of equity that pushes governments to reform their tax systems. It is going to be hard, but not reforming it would be even worse.

5.2. Third, *passive income* is the income generated from capital investments and can be divided into three categories of return: 1) dividends from shares and the like, 2) interest from bonds and the like, and 3) capital gains from the sale of shares or from the sale of bonds and the like. The mix is also known as income from the portfolio or, better, passive income, since the taxpayers neither control the source nor add personal energy to determine its production.

On the contrary, *active income* is (i) the income generated from employment performed under the direction of somebody else (i.e. wages and salaries), (ii) the income from self-employment or, last but not least, (iii) the income from business when a taxpayer entrepreneur combines labour and capital to set up his own organization to carry on an activity. Income from real estate is also generally deemed to be active income rather than passive income, since there is always an activity behind rental income.

The Report on Double Taxation of 1923 provides the "first bite to the apple" rule, under which the residence country should first "bite" passive income, while the source country should first "bite" active income. However, it is not always that clear when research and development in a country is an "activity" which might lead to the registration of patents & trademarks in another country and, from that moment on, to their possible "passive" exploitation all over the world. Income from exploitation (royalties) is indeed a hybrid between "active" and "passive", on which several countries may claim their power to tax.

5.3. *Double taxation* is a direct consequence of the state of residence applying a worldwide system and the State of source applying a territorial system. Since this is potentially creating a conflict with the ability to pay principle in the State of residence (no taxpayer should contribute to public expenses for more than his ability to pay), it is necessary to establish rules, or international tax principles, determining how the right to tax should be distributed between countries so as to limit the connections that give a country a legal right to tax. How to solve that juridical (or legal) double taxation is a matter of law, and the technical instruments are either the foreign tax credit or the exemption method.

The dark side of double taxation is represented by *double non-taxation,* that is, the situation in which the state of the source does not exercise the power to tax the income of non-resident taxpayers with the scope to attract their investments in the country, while the state of residence does not exercise the power to tax worldwide income with the scope to eliminate double taxation. A clear short circuit that the digitalization of the economy emphasizes by making it more difficult to fight such tax arbitration. Nobody complains about double non-taxation until there is sufficient revenue to finance public goods.

The single tax principle should be a reasonable compromise since it condemns both double taxation and double non-taxation and might be the future of international customary tax law. The residence jurisdiction should tax what is not taxed by the source jurisdiction, while the source jurisdiction should not reduce its withholding taxes unless residence-based taxation will apply. A single tax is not sufficient; a double tax is too much, although history demonstrates that the single tax principle can only be a trend.

5.4. Fourth, *benefit theory*, also known as the exchange theory of taxation, is generally linked to territorial systems, where taxes have often been understood as user charges. There are two forms of theory: 1) the cost theory, namely, taxes that are paid by non-resident taxpayers to cover the costs of their use of goods and services provided by the local government; and 2) the benefit theory, with taxes paid in accordance with the benefits conferred upon individuals. Neither cost theory nor benefit theory can avoid or solve the problem of international taxation.

On the other hand, there is a theory that is more comprehensive than the preceding one, since it includes what there is of value in the benefit theory. Redistributive taxation is linked to worldwide systems, and taxes are applied to resident taxpayers based on their ability to pay and have the main scope to redistribute resources among individuals of the social community. The fight between benefit and redistributive taxation is a never-ending story with no clear winner, although in the international context, benefit theory seems to prevail because it is the best language to speak for a taxpayer not belonging to the foreign hosting social community.

The combination of benefit theory with the single tax principle could bring to an international tax regime where double taxation and double non-taxation are avoided by: 1) assigning to the source jurisdiction the right to tax active business income and to the residence jurisdiction the right to tax passive portfolio income; and 2) allowing the other jurisdiction (residence for active, source for passive) to tax that income if the primary taxing jurisdiction refrains from taxing it. This should result in all income and capital being taxed once.

Redistributive theory is the other side of benefit theory and predicts that as inequality increases, political demand for revenue redistribution should also increase, especially in democratic settings. However, real-life complexities often distort this outcome, making redistribution a deeply political and contested process.

5.5. The last philosophical issue of international taxation relates to *tax competition* and its dark side—strange but true—to tax cooperation. The other way around happens if cooperation comes to mind first when thinking about international relations: tax competition would then be its dark side. The current age of globalization has brought capital to be much more mobile than labour, and its mobility has resulted in international tax competition in which sovereign States aim to attract either the portfolio capital of individuals or paper profits of multinational or foreign direct investments by lowering their tax rates on income earned by non-resident taxpayers. Beneficial tax competition occurs when general tax reductions apply to all taxpayers, residents and non-residents, while harmful tax competition, or better discriminatory tax competition, happens when tax reductions are granted only to non-resident investors. Harmful tax competition includes both production and headquarters tax havens, since they are typically granted to multinationals. It includes reductions in withholding taxes that are aimed solely at attracting foreign capital, unless measures are taken to ensure residence-based taxation. Finally, discriminatory tax competition includes traditional offshore tax havens with a low or zero tax rate if the tax base is confined almost entirely to non-resident investors.

The dark side of tax competition is *tax cooperation,* where countries belonging to the international community cooperate with each other to fight harmful tax competition and restore a climate of justice in international taxation. Understanding the functional and normative goals underlying nation-states' claims for tax sovereignty can enable them to assess, predict and influence prospects for tax cooperation. Any nation should take the responses of foreign governments into account when making international tax policies and as a reminder that cooperative multilateral policy-making may benefit both domestic and foreign taxpayers. However, there is no clear example of multilateralism's success, and this noble intention remains dark so far; tax justice remains an illusion, and hypocrisy proves to be the taxmaker.

References

Avi-Yona RS (2015) Who invented the Single Tax principle? An essay on the history of US Treaty Policy. NYU Law School Law Rev 59:305

Cappelen AW (2001) The moral rationale for international fiscal law. Ethics Int Aff 15:1

Clifton Fleming J Jr, Peroni RJ, Shay SE (2001) Fairness in international taxation: the ability-to-pay case for taxing worldwide income. Florida Tax Rev 5:4

Dodge JM (2004–2005) Theories of tax justice: ruminations on the benefit, partnership, and ability-to-pay principle. Tax Law Rev 58:399

Doernberg RL (2012) International taxation in a nutshell, 9th ed., West Nutshell Series

Garavan C (2023) The membership theory of taxation. Intertax 51(4)

Groves HM (1974) Tax philosophers: two hundred years of thought in Great Britain and the United States. University of Wisconsin Press

Kaufman NH (1998) Fairness and the taxation of international income. Law Policy Int Bus 29:145

Kern A (2020) Illusions of justice in international taxation. Philos Public Aff 48(2)

OECD (2019) Tax morale: what drives people and businesses to pay tax? Paris

Schoen W (2023) Is everybody obliged to pay taxes somewhere? Max Planck Institute for Tax Law and Public Finance Working Paper 2023-09, July 2023

Seligman ERA (1909) Progressive taxation in theory and practice. Princeton University Press

Smith A (1868) An inquiry into the nature and causes of the wealth of nations, (first edition 1776), edited by Edwin Cannan. Chicago University Press

Chapter 3
Politics of International Taxation

Contents

3.1 No Taxation Without Representation

Article 12 of the British Magna Carta provides that "Nullum scutagium vel auxilium ponatur in regno nostro" and was established on 15 June 1215 when barons proposed a strong need for checks and balances to express that King John was not above the law. Montesquieu explained the separation of powers in his major work "The Spirit of the Laws" (De l'esprit des lois, 1748) where He divided government into three parts—one to make laws, one to enforce them, and one to judge them—so no single person or group can control everything. The English version, "No taxation without representation", became a political slogan during the Enlightenment era as one of the major causes of the American and French Revolutions. Every modern constitution contains a reference to that commitment as an example of sovereignty that combines "territory, people and government".

"Taxes are the price we pay for a civilized society" was the dissenting opinion of Oliver Wendell Holmes Jr, Associate Justice of the US Supreme Court and Weld Professor of Law at the Harvard Law School, in the 1927 case *Compania General De Tabacos De Filipinas v. Collector of Internal Revenue* (275 US 87, 100) and is now carved over the entrance of the Internal Revenue Service building at 1111 Constitution Avenue of Washington, D.C.

G. Marino, *The Dark Side of International Tax Law*,
https://doi.org/10.1007/978-3-032-08159-9_3

Taxation is deeply political. Who must pay that price, how much, and what is the extent of civilization required? These are at the heart of politics itself. In essence, tax policy in the US provides a fair contribution to the protection of private property rights. Reference is to the work of philosophers L. Murphy and T. Nagel ("The Myth of Ownership, Taxes and Justice", Oxford University Press, 2002), who write that ownership comes to seem the most natural thing in the world. However, the modern economy in which we earn our salaries, own our homes, bank accounts, retirement savings, and personal possessions, and in which we can use our resources to consume or invest, would be impossible without the framework provided by the government, supported by taxes. In Europe, tax policy includes the protection of human rights, as Frans Vanistendael supports ("Legal Framework for Human Rights and Taxation in Europe", European Taxation, 1996). Rights are always duties in disguise.

There are several reasons for analysing international taxation from the perspective of political science. The liberalization of capital movement (Sinn 1991) and the increasing mobility of skilled labour (Tanzi 1994) represent an objective threat to the link between taxation and representation. In the most extreme scenario, capital income taxes will be lowered, perhaps to zero, by the dynamics of tax competition, and governments will be obliged to impose an increasing tax burden on unskilled labour and real estate properties, which are the only two immobile factors in a deeply integrated economy. The digital economy is exacerbating the idea of States having no power to tax multinational enterprises, whose burden is shifted onto the shoulders of middle-class workers, while a strong political lobby helps in keeping such a distance (Philippon 2019).

Also, the philosophical combination of worldwide versus territorial taxation, economic versus political allegiance, and benefit versus redistributive taxation may lead to political issues. A resident individual is generally taxed worldwide, but he will hardly be covered by public expenses of the State of residence when he happens to be outside its territory (i.e. legal and technical business infrastructure, military protection, passport and embassy services) unless he is also a citizen of that State. That same individual pays taxes worldwide but does not have voting rights in the State of residence unless he is also a citizen of that State. Last but not least, that same individual may receive political worldwide protection only from the State of citizenship, where he may eventually pay no taxes at all. If this is true, then only taxation based on citizenship seems to simultaneously satisfy the benefit and redistributive principles at the same time. The United States is the sole industrialized country that taxes based on citizenship, which is a deep political message to the world.

The conundrum of how to balance the desire to prevent both double taxation and complete tax avoidance by sustaining the competitive position of the domestic business is at the basis of the politics in international taxation of any developed country. The emphasis shifts from source to residence, from residence to source and back to residence again, depending also on economic events, multinational enterprises' decisions and mass media communications.

3.2 No Representation Without Taxation

The 2008 financial crisis, as well as several international tax evasion and fraud leak scandals (LGT, UBS, HSBC, Lux Leaks, Panama Papers and Paradise Papers), have created the conditions for some increased measure of coordination among countries in the field of public finance and international taxation, and "No representation without taxation" seems to be the new paradigm to consider. Nevertheless, as of the same period, digitalization and international tax planning have created loopholes, allowing multinational tech companies to escape taxes everywhere, even though personal tax has increased, and the coronavirus crisis has made the reform of international tax standards more urgent than ever. Nearly one-third of the companies that received coronavirus loans from the Bank of England are either based in or substantially owned by a tax-haven resident, according to TaxWatch UK, a think tank. Baker Hughes, a GE subsidiary, was granted a £600 million loan despite its parent company being sued by the UK over the unpaid tax going back 16 years.

3.3 Representation Without Taxation

There are two more paradigms to complete the politics of international taxation. One is "Representation without taxation" and is tailored to the European Union as a supranational organization where the European Parliament represents all European citizens with zero power to tax, that being only with the Council of the European Union (also called the Council of Ministers) that is the body of European governments, different from the European Council (setting the EU's overall political direction and priorities). For most tax matters (like VAT rules, corporate taxation, and excise duties) the Council of the EU must decide unanimously—all Member States must agree. The European Commission proposes tax legislation (executive role) while the European Parliament is only consulted but does not co-legislate on taxes. This is indeed the largest weakness of constitutional architecture since it is impossible to build European public goods like defence, transportation, healthcare and justice to favour the internal market. Even God decided that his representative on earth, the Pope, must be elected by a majority and not by unanimity, as of the Third Lateran Council back in 1179, convened by Pope Alexander III.

3.4 Taxation Without Representation

However, there is a last paradigm that is of growing importance and brings the name of "Taxation without representation". It was tailored by the Organization for Economic Co-operation and Development (OECD), first founded as the Organization for European Economic Co-operation (OEEC) in 1948 to monitor the Marshall Plan and then transformed in 1961 to open access to non-European countries. The OECD is an intergovernmental organisation, its members are represented by their governments—not by private companies or non-state actors, and decisions are taken by consensus (all member governments must agree, or at least not object). Today, the OECD is the Club of rich countries and is no longer just producing soft laws, but it is also supporting the adoption of a multilateral convention (MLI) to implement measures against aggressive tax planning. The moral suasion that the OECD exercised on its members, other than the US, and on non-OECD countries to adopt the Global Minimum Tax (GMT) as a global standard solution for a level playing field in tax competition has been the demonstration that philosophy, politics and economics (PPE) of international taxation may prevail over any domestic legislative procedure. This questions the legitimacy of the OECD as a new Authority for global tax governance and the economic pressure that it could create on a single State, jeopardizing the compatibility of domestic tax decision-making policy with the constitutional principles usually applicable in the legal systems of democratic sovereign States. Bertil Wiman, in his Klaus Vogel Lecture 2022, raised the issue on who should be in the driver's seat in developing international tax norms, civil servants or national parliaments?

References

Dietsch P (2011) Rethinking sovereignty in international fiscal policy. Rev Int Stud 37:2107–2120

Dourado AP (2024) Legitimacy and validity of tax law in an international context. Intertax 52(3)

Draghi M (2024) A competitiveness strategy for Europe

European Commission, Business Taxation for the 21st Century, COM(2021) 251 final

European Commission, Towards a More Efficient and Democratic Decision Making in EU Tax Policy, COM(2019) 8 final

Final Report and Recommendations of the High-Level Group on Own Resources, Future Financing of the EU, 2016

Motala M (2016) The new global politics of sovereign international tax: space, time, and why BEPS is not the final frontier, SSRN, August 1st, 2016

Murphy L, Nagel T (2002) The myth of ownership, taxes and justice. Oxford University Press

Philippon T (2019), The great reversal: how America gave up on free markets, Harvard University Press.

Sinn HW, The non-neutrality of inflation for international capital movements. European economic review, 35, 1, 1991.

Sydanmaanlakka L (2024) Power and expertise in global tax governance. Intertax 52(3)

Tanzi V (1994), Taxation in an integrating world, Brookings Institution Press, Washington DC.

van der Vlugt S (2023) The principle of legality of taxation as a general principle of EU law: national and supranational differences of interpretation and potential difficulties. EC Tax Rev 5

Chapter 4
Economics of International Taxation

Contents

4.1 The International Tax Neutrality

The mantra is "pecunia non olet" or, alternatively, cash is always king, and there is a way to justify worldwide or territorial taxation stronger than the philosophical inter-individual and international equity principle, through capital export neutrality (CEN) and capital import neutrality (CIN).

CEN requires that a resident taxpayer of any country pays the same marginal rate of income taxation, regardless of the country in which he invests his capital. CEN is not only neutral about where such investments are made but also is indifferent about which country produces income for another. Typically, economists regard CEN as essential for worldwide economic efficiency, because the location of investments would be unaffected by capital income taxes that must always be paid in the State of residence of the investor but would only be selected based on its social and economic infrastructure that could maximize the return on investment. The location par excellence has a name: the United States—and the CEN supporters come from there.

CIN is a second kind of neutrality that requires all investments in a given country to pay the same marginal rate of income taxation, regardless of the residence of the investor. CIN thus subjects all business activities within a specific country to the same level of taxation, whether the activity is conducted by a resident or a non-resident taxpayer. If CIN holds, all savers, regardless of their residence, receive the same after-tax return. They, therefore, face the same prices for future versus present consumption, and the allocation of savings is efficient. The best location, in that

G. Marino, *The Dark Side of International Tax Law*,
https://doi.org/10.1007/978-3-032-08159-9_4

case, is the source country rather than the residence country; to make it simpler, it is the rest of the world rather than the United States.

The economic discussion on international taxation is ever dominated by a simple matrix, where capital export neutrality and capital import neutrality generally constitute the normative universe. Implementing these policies requires worldwide taxation with foreign tax credit or territorial taxation with foreign earnings exempt from tax. In theory, CEN gives the prime claim to tax internationally to the country of residence, and CIN awards that right to the country of source.

4.2 The Economic Double Taxation

Double taxation has been anticipated as a philosophical issue of international taxation that imposes on sovereign States the need to find a solution not to violate the constitutional principle that every taxpayer has to contribute to public expenses not beyond his ability to pay taxes, and either the foreign tax credit method or the exemption method helps to solve the legal double taxation.

However, there is another kind of double taxation that occurs when two different taxpayers pay two different taxes on the same income flow. That is the case of the economic double taxation resulting from the combination of the individual income tax on dividends distributed out of business profits already subject to corporate income tax.

Taxes on corporations are: (i) desirable to collect public revenue in ways that would improve the economic well-being, not harm the economic well-being, or impose costs on those beyond the political pale; (ii) necessary as an essential component of any adequate system of personal taxation and (iii) convenient since they are imposed at a "conduit" level that makes it virtually inconceivable not to do so.

The international tax relationship between individuals, as well as corporate shareholders and their corporations, is more crucial for economists than for jurists and adds some complication to the discussion of worldwide versus territorial taxation. Indeed, if the economic double taxation is not solved both at a domestic and international level, no investor, whether individual or corporation, would inject their money into a corporation. While there are different approaches to economic double taxation at the level of individual shareholders and related corporations—leaving the issue unsolved (e.g. the US)—most countries tend to eliminate economic double taxation between parent companies and controlled subsidiaries to allow the multinational enterprises to grow in dimension. The tax regime of the relationship between individual investors and their shareholdings may drive to different macroeconomic consequences. In the US, for example, for an individual investor holding shares in a company listed at the NYSE, long-term capital gains are usually taxed at lower rates than ordinary dividends, and this leads the corporate management to offer the financial community more emphasis on business expectations, raising up the shares for buy-back, rather than focusing on real profits. It was the case with the birth of internet in the late nineties of the last century (with the related financial bubble) and it is now the case with the artificial intelligence potential applications, shares values raise beyond any actual real profit.

Last but not least, on the other hand, corporations and similar structures for high-net-worth individuals (i.e. family offices, trusts, foundations and the like) may also act as "tax stoppers", bringing *de facto* double non-taxation. In particular, it must be understood whether corporations and similar structures are *real* interpositions between the taxpayers and their assets, in which case some anti-tax avoidance regimes may apply to pierce the corporate veil, make them transparent and impute the income tax to the individuals in their State of residence (i.e. shell companies or closely held corporations), or whether corporations and similar structures are *fictitious* interpositions between the taxpayers and their assets, in which case criminal tax investigations may arise to recover income taxes as well as to re-educate individuals by way of depriving them of personal freedom. A triangle is the best geometrical expression in international taxation.

References

Bird RM (2002) Why tax corporations?, Bull Int Tax, 5, 2002

Graetz MJ (2001) The David R. Tillinghast Lecture – taxing international income: inadequate principles, outdated concepts, and unsatisfactory policies. Tax Law Rev 54:261

Graetz MJ (2003) Foundations of international income taxation. Foundation Press

Musgrave R (1959) The theory of public finance: a study in public economy,. McGraw-Hill

Richman PB (in Musgrave) (1964) Taxation of foreign investment income. An economic analysis. Am Econ Rev 54(5)

Vogel K (1988) Worldwide vs. Source Taxation of Income: a review and re-evaluation of arguments (Part I). Intertax 16(8/9)

Chapter 5
History of International Taxation

Contents

5.1 History of International Taxation

The issue of international double taxation became evident after World War I, when the world was turning to high-income taxes to finance the war efforts. The result was an international financial conference held in Brussels in 1920 under the auspices of the newly formed International Chamber of Commerce, which called upon the League of Nations to address the double income taxation issue.

On 5 April 1923, four economists—professors Edwin Seligman and Josiah Stamp, representing two capital-exporting States (the United States and the United Kingdom, respectively), applying worldwide taxation and professors Luigi Einaudi and Gerardus Bruins, representing two capital-importing States (Italy and the Netherlands, respectively), applying territorial taxation—submitted a Report on double taxation to the Financial Committee of the newly formed League of Nations.

The Report first recognizes that between residence and source, the rights of the source country must prevail because income arises within the source country, and the residence country cannot prevent the source country from taxing that income. The solution is that the onus of preventing double taxation must fall on the residence country, and the methods to eliminate it are either (i) foreign tax credit by granting

G. Marino, *The Dark Side of International Tax Law*,
https://doi.org/10.1007/978-3-032-08159-9_5

a reduction in its own taxes equal to the foreign tax paid or (ii) the exemption method by refraining from taxing foreign source income.

The second contribution of the Report is the recognition of the benefit principle, under which active (business) income should be taxed primarily at source, while passive (investment) income should be taxed primarily on a residential basis. The reasoning behind this compromise is now obsolete, since the distinction between active and passive becomes more difficult every day. Nevertheless, it is the principle that underlies all tax treaties, which maintain the right of the source country to tax active income while shifting the tax on passive income to the residence country.

The Report is indeed a masterpiece in the field of international taxation of income and capital and culminated in the drafting of a Model Treaty in 1928 ("the 1928 Model Treaty"), which formed the basis of many bilateral tax treaties during the interwar period. This Model was used as a reference for negotiating bilateral treaties between countries, with the goal of preventing double income taxation and establishing shared rules for the taxation of cross-border income. As the distributed implications of the 1928 Model Treaty became increasingly tangible in source countries, collective action among Latin American countries accelerated. In 1943, the US and Canada agreed with Latin American countries on a "Mexico Draft" model convention that was largely based on the 1928 Model Treaty but granted source countries stronger taxing rights. After World War II, another model convention to govern bilateral treaties was drafted in 1946. This "London Model" also adhered to the 1928 Model Treaty and, in comparison, the primary difference with the Mexico Draft was the balance of taxing rights in favour of residence countries, ultimately winning the war. Ultimately, in 1963, the London draft served as the basis for the Organization for Economic Co-operation and Development's (OECD) Draft Double Tax Convention in 1977 (OECD Model Tax Convention [MTC]) and is currently the foundation of a network of more than 3000 bilateral tax treaties that incorporate its principles.

Even the origins of its opposite, that is, double non-taxation, can be found in that document, since stating that the State of residence adopts the tax credit method to resolve double taxation is like saying in an embryonic way that it also resolves double non-taxation (no tax, no credit).

1.1. In any case, it was another Report, on double taxation and evasion, presented in London on 12 April 1927 by another Commission of Technical Experts [Clavier (Belgium), Valnicek (Czechoslovakia), Baudouin-Bugnet (France), Thompson (Great Britain), D'Aroma (Italy), Damsté (Holland) and, finally, Blau (Switzerland)], which explicitly stated for the first time that: "From the very outset, [it was] realized the necessity of dealing with the questions of tax evasion and double taxation in co-ordination with each other. It is highly desirable that States should come to an agreement with a view to ensuring that a taxpayer shall not be taxed on the same income by a number of different countries, and it seems equally desirable that such international cooperation should prevent certain incomes from escaping taxation altogether. The most elementary and undisputed principles of fiscal justice, therefore, required that the experts should devise a scheme whereby all incomes would be taxed once and only once" (Double Taxation and Tax Evasion: Report; C. 216. M. 85, p. 23). In fact, one taxation is not enough, and double taxation is too much.

This statement, subsequently summarized by authoritative doctrine with the expression "single tax principle", was slow to gain ground, probably because it was not perceived as a solidarity-based problem of tax revenue within the international community, but rather it was handled on a case-by-case basis, and in an absolutely unilateral manner, by Nation-States from their perspective of source of income rather than residence of the recipient.

An example of this is American tax law when America was a land of conquest, which, in renegotiating some bilateral conventions (Luxembourg 1962, Netherlands/Netherlands Antilles 1963, Finland 1970, Iceland 1975, France 1978), prohibited reduced withholdings on dividends, interests and royalties paid to subjects who had exemption regimes in their States of residence. In particular, the Limitation on Benefits (LOB) clause was codified in the American model of bilateral convention to eliminate double taxation, according to which dividends, interests and royalties paid by taxpayers resident in the United States benefit from reduced conventional withholdings on exit, provided that the recipient companies meet the requirements of rootedness in the State of residence.

1.2. Only the 2008 financial crisis, combined with the globalization/digitalization of the economy and the overexposure of public debt of sovereign States grouped in the G20, created conditions of solidarity for them to ask the OECD to overcome the traditional considerations against double taxation dating back to the 1920s, and to go so far as to condemn double non-taxation as an equally distorting phenomenon of international relations, as emerged in the Base Erosion Profit Shifting (BEPS) Project of 2013, concluded in 2015, which was followed, for the Member States of the European Union, by Communication COM(2016) 23 final, from the Commission to the European Parliament and the Council on the anti-tax avoidance package; next steps to ensure effective taxation and greater tax transparency in the EU.

The nine decades that have passed between the 1923 Report and the BEPS Project have seen the perspective of international taxation change radically: if in the Introduction of the 1923 Report the question was posed, "Can any general principles be formulated as the basis for an international convention to remove the evil consequences of double taxation?", in the 2013 BEPS it is stated, "(...) the Action Plan identifies treaty abuse, and in particular treaty shopping, as one of the most important sources of BEPS concern".

However, it is important to underline that this change in perspective has also not meant a change in the underlying questions and issues. Luigi Einaudi and his illustrious colleagues in the second decade of the last century asked themselves, "(…) the point is that when the money has left the pocket of the individual, its destination is not a single one but is due to all those governments to whom the individual owes economic allegiance. How, then, should the sum that he finally pays reach these several governments which render him service? The problem consists in ascertaining where the true economic interests of the individual are found". This question is the most current one in the world of large corporations and the Internet, and it is also interesting to note how it was posed in the section of the Report dedicated to the "Doctrine of Economic Allegiance", which explores the criteria of connection and economic belonging of subjects and their activities to States.

The theory of economic allegiance, which outlines the main guidelines for the allocation of revenue from operations involving more than one jurisdiction, is based on three fundamental considerations aimed at finding solutions that reflect economic reality as closely as possible: (1) the *production* of wealth, (2) the *possession* of wealth and (3) the *disposition* of wealth. Then, as now, the focus was on finding solutions that would allow us to identify "where" wealth was produced and "by whom" it was owned and, ultimately, by whom and where it could be used. This research had to (or rather, must) then be integrated with a series of further considerations, this time of a more strictly tax nature, which produces a series of institutions that are still valid today and increasingly called into question by recent economic developments, in particular, "Residence and Domicile" and "Origin and Situs".

Even less has this change of perspective significantly contributed to the creation of international solidarity in combating the phenomenon of double non-taxation. The feeling is rather that each of the States is acting on stage so as not to contradict the OECD, but then behind the scenes, it goes ahead on its own, because those who do it themselves always do it for three.

These categories, presented in 1923, have contributed significantly to the evolution of modern tax systems, and once again, perhaps after having simply been renamed, they represent the core of the most current issues debated within the international scientific community, including the exchange of financial information.

1.3. After 90 years, in March 2013, the OECD released the Report "Base Erosion Profit Shifting" (BEPS), which represents the other edge of the international tax conundrum, being the double non-taxation of income. The Report is divided into three areas and consists of 15 Actions: 1) the area of "coherence", according to which tax laws of different countries should work so that all income falls under the jurisdiction of at least one tax authority and at most one (actions 1–5); 2) the area of "substance", according to which where income is taxed should align with the substance of how and where the people responsible for creating value actually operate (actions 6–10); and, last but not least, 3) the area of "transparency", according to which all relevant tax authorities should have data on the taxpayer's global activities, with the expectation that this will make it easier to determine whether they are paying their "fair share" in a given jurisdiction (actions 11–15).

To overcome this challenge, the OECD developed the umbrella of a Multilateral Instrument, a treaty mechanism capable of modifying existing bilateral tax treaties without renegotiating each one. The Multilateral Instrument (MLI) was opened for signature in June 2017 and has since been signed by over 100 jurisdictions, covering more than 1800 tax treaties. The innovation lies in its ability to function as a layer of interpretation and amendment applied to pre-existing treaties, thereby transforming them in line with the BEPS recommendations.

The MLI is notable for its flexibility and scalability, built around a modular approach that respects national sovereignty while promoting international alignment. Countries can choose which tax treaties to modify (their "Covered Tax Agreements") and which MLI provisions to adopt, provided that they meet the minimum standards required by the BEPS framework.

- Minimum Standards: Certain provisions are mandatory, such as those related to preventing treaty abuse (BEPS Action 6) and enhancing dispute resolution mechanisms (BEPS Action 14).
- Optional Provisions and Reservations: States may opt out of specific clauses or choose alternative methods of implementation. For instance, they may select between a Principal Purpose Test (PPT) or a Limitation on Benefits (LOB) clause to address treaty shopping.
- Matching Mechanism: A treaty is only modified if both parties agree to apply the same MLI provision. This system ensures clarity and predictability, even within a highly flexible structure.

Unlike traditional treaties that replace or rewrite existing texts, the MLI modifies the legal effect of the provisions in existing treaties. This is done through a process of dynamic interpretation in which the MLI provisions apply "as if" they were part of the underlying treaty. This allows countries to preserve their existing treaty networks while upgrading them to meet modern anti-avoidance standards.

In 2017, the G20, an international forum that brought together the world's major economies, adopted the idea of global tax reform and tasked the OECD with developing a framework for a fairer international taxation system, which included a global minimum tax, BEPS 2.0. After years of negotiations, in 2021, over 130 countries reached a historic agreement on the global minimum tax under the aegis of the OECD. The agreement sets a minimum tax rate of 15% on multinationals with global revenues exceeding 750 million euros. This measure has been hailed as a significant step towards greater tax fairness at the international level. The agreement was then ratified at the national level by the participating countries, with implementation scheduled for 2024. The goal is to ensure that all multinational corporations pay at least 15% in taxes, regardless of where they are located or where they register their profits.

While Europe was very quick to implement such a complex minimum standard, the Trump Administration rejected it, leaving the international community with a chaotic feeling.

5.2 History of the US International Taxation

In the 1923–2023 century, it is worth periodizing the history of US international taxation that has influenced other tax systems as well as the works of international organizations. Reuven Avi-Yonah has initially distinguished four ages: 1) *the age of benefits* (1918–1960), driven by Prof. Thomas Adams, Prof. Edwin Seligman and

Prof. Mitchell Carroll, with the dominance of the "economic allegiance" as benefit-based concept used to justify both source-based taxation (the "production of wealth") as well as residence-based taxation (the "possession of wealth" and "disposition of wealth"); 2) *the age of neutrality* (1961–1980) driven by professors Stanley Surrey, David Tillinghast, Paul McDaniel and Hugh Ault, who sponsored the economic concept of efficiency, which in the international context translated into neutrality (in particular, capital export neutrality) that is the main reason behind Subpart F 1962 legislation on Controlled Foreign Corporations (CFC) of President Kennedy; 3) *the age of competition* (1981–1997), driven by Charles McLure, David Rosenbloom and Michael Graetz, who sponsored the idea that in an era of increasing globalization, the US should pay more attention to competitiveness of its multinationals in the face of increasing foreign competition. In addition, the need to attract increasingly mobile foreign capital led the US to reduce source-based taxation of foreign investment income, while at the same time the increased emphasis on source taxation and budgetary pressures led to increased source-based taxation of business income; and, last but not least, 4) *the age of cooperation* (1998–today) starting with two main decisions of the Clinton Administration (i) to enact the Internet Tax Freedom Act (21 October 1998) establishing federal policy regarding Federal and State taxation of the Internet, based upon its unique characteristics as a mode of interstate and global trade uniquely susceptible to multiple and discriminatory taxation, and (ii) to cooperate with the OECD's harmful tax competition initiative from 1998 onwards. This period is marked by a different response to globalization than to unilateral competition, acting in concert with the US's major trading partners to reduce both double taxation and double non-taxation. A turning date to remember is 2 April 2009, after the 2008 US financial crisis, when the G20 met in London and launched the global war against tax evasion, aiming to fight offshore countries to collect the necessary revenue to rescue the US banking system.

Although this last age of cooperation has the potential of beginning a truly different approach to integrating the US and international tax regimes, the 2008 US financial crisis and the Great Recession led to millions losing their jobs and homes and brought a political reaction on both sides of the Atlantic with Brexit, on one side, and the election of Donald Trump on the other side. The Nation State is reasserting itself, and one of the instruments it uses is taxation. "America first" and "Make America Great Again" of the Trump Administration risk curbing this trend due to the different interests in the taxation of the digital economy driven by the super-powerful US techoligarchy.

5.3 History of International Taxation Through International Organizations

Another perspective is to look at international taxation through the history of the international organizations that have each played significant roles in the evolution of international tax standards, cooperation and regulation, namely the Organization for Economic Co-operation and Development (OECD), the United Nations (UN), and the World Trade Organization (WTO).

The OECD has been a central actor in the development of international tax policies since its formation in 1961. As a forum for the governments of industrialized countries, the OECD has focused on promoting economic growth and stability, which includes addressing issues related to taxation. One of the OECD's most significant contributions to international taxation is the development of the Model Tax Convention (MTC). This model serves as a template for bilateral tax treaties aimed at preventing double taxation and tax evasion. It provides guidelines on how income and profits should be allocated between jurisdictions and how taxes should be applied to cross-border transactions. The OECD has recently published the 2025 update to the OECD MTC including the changes to the Commentary on Article 5 relating to "home office" permanent establishment.

In the 1990s, the OECD began addressing the challenges posed by harmful tax competition and tax havens, which led in 1998 to the creation of the "Harmful Tax Practices Initiative". This initiative sought to curb practices that eroded tax bases and distorted trade and investment flows.

The OECD's most ambitious and influential project in recent years has been the "Base Erosion and Profit Shifting (BEPS) Project", launched in 2013 to solve the double non-taxation problem led by the rapid digitalization of the economy. BEPS project 1.0 addresses tax avoidance strategies that exploit gaps and mismatches in tax rules to artificially shift profits to low- or no-tax locations. The OECD's BEPS Action Plan has led to the adoption of 15 actions designed to ensure that profits are taxed where economic activities generating profits are performed and where value is created. The BEPS 1.0 initiative has become a cornerstone of global tax governance, influencing both national tax reforms and international tax treaties.

Despite these achievements, BEPS 1.0 did not reach enough consensus, and in October 2021, BEPS 2.0 was launched by the OECD with the G20, consisting of Pillar 1, designed to address the problem of taxing corporate income at source in accordance with the benefit principle, while Pillar 2 directly implemented the single tax principle by ensuring a minimal level of tax in the residence jurisdictions if the source country tax is not sufficient, and if that is not enough, by ensuring a minimal level of tax in the source jurisdiction if the residence country tax is insufficient.

The international tax results of BEPS 2.0 are still to come due to the strong opposition of the United States.

3.1. The United Nations has played a critical role in addressing the concerns of developing countries in the field of international taxation. Unlike the OECD, which primarily represents the interests of developed countries, the UN has sought to provide a more balanced approach that considers the needs of both developed and developing nations.

The UN Model Double Taxation Convention between Developed and Developing Countries is one of the UN's key contributions. It serves as an alternative to the OECD Model, giving more taxing rights to source countries (where income is generated) rather than residence countries (where the income earner resides). This is particularly important for developing countries that often rely on source-based taxation to secure revenue from foreign investments and operations within their borders.

In recent years, the UN has also focused on issues such as taxation of the digital economy and the role of taxation in achieving the Sustainable Development Goals (SDGs). The UN Committee of Experts on International Cooperation in Tax Matters plays a pivotal role in fostering dialogue and cooperation regarding tax issues, particularly in promoting fair and effective tax systems in developing countries. The Resolution adopted by the UN General Assembly in 2023 to proceed with the option to develop a framework convention on international tax cooperation may lead to a new stage for the international tax regime that evolved from the work of the League of Nations pre-World War II and was fully developed under the strong hand of the OECD after the war. The UN Framework on International Tax Cooperation is a proposed global treaty aims to provide a more inclusive, fair and cooperative system for international taxation and is meant to complement (or in some views challenge) the existing tax-governance arrangements, such as those developed under the OECD framework. This initiative could mark a major shift in global tax governance, moving from a patchwork of bilateral treaties and voluntary cooperation to a universal, binding framework embraced by a broad majority of countries, although it remains a work in progress since much depends on the outcome of the negotiations (2025–2027) and whether a critical mass of countries signs and implements it.

3.2. While the World Trade Organization (WTO) is primarily concerned with regulating international trade, it has also indirectly influenced international taxation, particularly through its rules on the trade-related aspects of taxation.

The WTO's "Agreement on Subsidies and Countervailing Measures (SCM)" and the "General Agreement on Tariffs and Trade (GATT)" include provisions that address the tax treatment of exports and imports. For example, the WTO prohibits certain types of tax incentives considered export subsidies, as these can distort trade by providing unfair advantages to domestic producers. Additionally, WTO rules have implications for Value Added Tax (VAT) and customs duties, as they require non-discriminatory treatment of imported goods.

One significant case highlighting the interaction between trade and tax policies is the "Foreign Sales Corporation (FSC) case", brought by the European Union against the United States in the late 1990s. The WTO ruled that the US tax provisions that provided tax benefits to exporters through Foreign Sales Corporations were an illegal export subsidy under WTO rules. This case underscores how the WTO discipline can influence national tax policies, particularly in areas where tax and trade issues intersect. Within the new international order, it must be observed the disinterest of the United States to multilateralism in favour of bilateralism. This brings to the leadership of China within many international organizations (i.e. UNESCO, FAO, WB, and IMF).

3.3. The International Chamber of Commerce (ICC), founded in 1919, has also played a pivotal yet often underappreciated role in the development of the modern international tax system. As a global organization representing business interests across borders, the ICC acted as a bridge between private enterprises and international policymaking, particularly in the formative years of tax cooperation under the League of Nations and, later, during the evolution of OECD frameworks. Its involvement has influenced the design of international tax norms, particularly in relation to double taxation, tax treaties, and transfer pricing principles.

While it is not a regulatory body, the ICC has played a foundational and ongoing role in shaping the international tax landscape. From its collaboration with the League of Nations in the 1920s to its participation in today's global tax debates, the ICC has acted as the voice of business, promoting a balanced approach to taxation—one that encourages cross-border investment while supporting international efforts to combat avoidance and ensure fairness. Its legacy is embedded in the very structure of the global tax treaty network and continues to evolve in step with the demands of a digitized, globalized economy.

5.4 History of European Taxation

The history of taxation within the European Union (EU) is deeply intertwined with the broader evolution of the Union's constitutional architecture and the challenges it faces. From its inception, the EU's approach to taxation has been marked by the tension between the sovereignty of individual Member States and the push for greater integration to ensure the proper functioning of the internal market.

The Treaty of Rome (1957), which laid the groundwork for the European Economic Community (EEC), established the principle of unanimity in tax matters. This reflected the deep sensitivity surrounding national fiscal sovereignty. Taxation, being a core element of State sovereignty, was an area where Member States were particularly reluctant to cede power. Consequently, any decision regarding tax harmonization required the unanimous agreement of all Member States.

This requirement for unanimity has proven to be one of the most significant structural flaws in the EU's constitutional architecture. The unanimity rule has made it exceedingly difficult to achieve meaningful tax harmonization, as any single Member State can veto proposed changes. This has led to a fragmented tax landscape within the EU, with significant variations in corporate tax rates, VAT systems, and other tax policies across Member States. Such disparities have often resulted in distortions within the internal market, tax competition, and, in some cases, aggressive tax planning by multinational corporations exploiting the differences between national tax systems.

Strange but true, a positive evolution within the European house has to do with the creation of a common set of administrative rules for tax cooperation among Member States that hopefully will lead to a real European Tax Agency much earlier than a common direct taxation.

Amidst the challenges posed by the unanimity requirement, the European Court of Justice (ECJ) has played a pivotal and transformative role in advancing tax integration within the EU. The ECJ has consistently upheld the application of the EU's fundamental freedoms—such as the free movement of goods, services, capital, and people—to the realm of taxation.

Through its jurisprudence, the ECJ has effectively acted as a catalyst for tax harmonization even in the absence of political agreements among Member States. The Court has struck down national tax laws that it deems to be in violation of EU law, particularly those that create barriers to cross-border economic activities or discriminate against non-residents. For example, the ECJ has ruled against national tax measures that restrict the free movement of capital or provide preferential tax treatment to domestic companies over foreign entities.

These decisions have had a profound impact on the tax policies of Member States, often forcing them to amend their laws to comply with EU principles. The ECJ's decisions have thus served as a de facto mechanism for harmonizing aspects of tax law across the EU, despite the lack of unanimity among Member States. A recent example is represented by the saga of preferential tax rulings given by certain Member States to multinational corporations (Apple Ireland Case C-465/20P (2024), while for Amazon Luxembourg, Fiat Finance & Trade Luxembourg and Starbucks Netherlands, after rulings by the lower courts (General Court), the Commission formally closed the investigations (on 28th November 2024) and concluded that the tax rulings did not constitute unlawful state aid, effectively ending those cases).

The tension between the need for tax harmonization and the principle of national sovereignty remains a central challenge for the EU. While the ECJ has made significant strides in promoting the application of fundamental freedoms to tax matters, the underlying issue of unanimity continues to hinder more comprehensive reforms. Strange but true, the European Union finds unanimity in taxation only when there is international external pressure, as is the case of US Foreign Account Tax Compliance Act (FATCA) that led to the automatic exchange of information through the Directive on Administrative Cooperation in Tax Matters, BEPS 1.0 that led to the Anti-Tax Avoidance Directive (ATAD) to align the European tax systems with the 15 Actions, and BEPS 2.0 that led to the introduction of the Global Minimum Tax Directive well in advance in comparison with other countries of the international community. On the other side, the recent debates around the introduction of the European digital service tax to fight the US technoligarchy superpower, as well as discussions on a common consolidated corporate tax base (CCCTB), have highlighted the difficulties of achieving unanimity when the European Union needs to find unilaterally its proper tax identity.

In conclusion, the history of EU taxation reflects both the strengths and weaknesses of the Union's constitutional framework. The rule of unanimity, while respecting national sovereignty, has often led to deadlock and inefficiencies. At the same time, the European Court of Justice has played a crucial role in pushing for greater integration by ensuring that national tax policies do not undermine the fundamental freedoms that underpin the EU's internal market. Moving forward, the EU will need to navigate these challenges carefully if it is to achieve a more coherent and effective tax policy framework.

5.5 History of Italian International Taxation

The history of international taxation in the Italian tax system reflects the broader evolution of Italy's approach to economic integration and globalization, as well as its responses to changes in the global and European tax landscape. This history is particularly marked by a significant shift in the 1970s from a territorial tax system to a worldwide tax system and by Italy's consistent position as a "follower" in the context of tax competition within Europe.

Before the 1970s, Italy's tax system operated predominantly on a territorial basis. Under this system, Italy taxed only the income generated within its borders, regardless of whether it was earned by residents or non-residents. This approach was in line with the tax practices of many countries at the time, where the focus was on taxing income where it was earned, rather than where the taxpayer was domiciled or resident.

The 1970s marked a significant turning point in Italy's approach to taxation, driven by the increasing complexity of international trade and finance, as well as the growing need for alignment with global tax standards. During this period, Italy transitioned from a territorial to a worldwide tax system. This meant that Italian residents, both individuals and corporations, were subject to taxation on their global income, regardless of where that income was earned.

This shift was part of a broader international trend towards worldwide taxation, as countries sought to prevent tax avoidance and evasion by ensuring that their residents could not simply shift income to low-tax jurisdictions. The worldwide tax system aimed to capture income that might otherwise escape taxation under a purely territorial regime.

Italy's adoption of the worldwide tax system was also influenced by the growing importance of international agreements, particularly double taxation treaties. These treaties, designed to prevent the same income from being taxed in multiple jurisdictions, became an integral part of Italy's international tax policy, balancing the interests of securing tax revenues with the need to avoid double taxation that could hinder cross-border economic activities.

Throughout the subsequent decades, as European integration deepened, Italy consistently positioned itself as a "follower" rather than a leader in the realm of tax competition. Unlike some European countries, such as the Netherlands, Luxembourg and Ireland, which adopted aggressive tax policies to attract multinational corporations, Italy largely refrained from engaging in such practices.

Several factors contributed to Italy's follower position as Cinderella: 1) Conservative Fiscal Policy. Italy's approach to tax policy has generally been conservative, focusing on maintaining a relatively stable tax base rather than competing aggressively for foreign investment through tax incentives. This has been partly due to the country's large public debt and the need to secure steady revenue streams. 2) Alignment with European Directives. Italy has often waited for a broader European or OECD consensus before making significant changes to its tax system. This cautious approach reflects Italy's preference for aligning itself with international standards, rather than setting them. For example, Italy has been supportive of EU-wide initiatives to fight tax avoidance and has implemented various anti-avoidance measures in line with OECD guidelines, such as the Base Erosion and Profit Shifting (BEPS) project. 3) Economic Structure. Italy's economic structure, characterized by a large number of small and medium-sized enterprises (SMEs) and a relatively smaller presence of multinational corporations, has meant that the country's tax policy has been less focused on attracting large international firms compared to countries like the Netherlands or Ireland.

In recent years, Italy has faced increasing pressure to modernize its tax system in response to global developments, such as digitalization and the rise of the digital economy. The country has implemented various reforms to align with EU directives and international standards, including measures to tackle tax avoidance and evasion.

Despite these efforts, Italy continues to grapple with the challenges of maintaining a competitive tax environment while securing adequate revenue to support its public finances. The country remains a follower in the ongoing discussions around global tax reform, including the OECD's initiatives on taxing the digital economy and establishing a global minimum tax. The last tax reform of 2023 of Vice minister of finance Maurizio Leo is still ongoing and represents a great challenge for the Italian tax system to achieve a pivotal role in the international tax community, especially for the tax regime of high-net-worth individuals (HNWIs) and for the cooperative tax compliance programs of multinational enterprises.

References

Adams C (2001) For good and evil, the impact of taxes on the course of civilization. Madison Books edition

Avi-Yonah RS (2023a) The 1923 Report and the International Tax Revolution. Intertax 51(5)

Avi-Yonah RS (2023b) Nothing new under the sun? The historical origins of the benefit principle. Intertax 51(8/9)

Avi-Yonah RS (2024) The four ages of US international taxation revisited. U. of Michigan Public Law research Paper Forthcoming, 30 June 2024

Bank SA, Stark KJ (eds) (2005) Business tax stories. Foundation Press

Huret RD (2014) American tax resisters, Harvard University Press.

Jogarajan S (2018) Double taxation and the league of nations. Cambridge University Press

Jogarajan S (2020) The 100th anniversary of international institutions and international taxation. Intertax 48(10)

Keen M, Slemrod J (2021) Rebellion, rascals, and revenue. Princeton University Press

League of Nations, Report on Double Taxation, April 5th 1923
Savitskiy A (2021) The first tax treaties: in search of origins. Intertax 49(6/7)
Seligman ERA (2012) The income tax, a study of the history, theory, and practice of income taxation at home and abroad, (first edition 1914) Forgotten Books edition
Simons HC (1932) Personal income taxation: the definition of income as a problem of fiscal policy. University of Chicago Press
Stewart M (2022) Tax and government in the 21st century. Cambridge University Press
Teo NJ (2023) The United Nations in Global Tax Coordination. Cambridge University Press
Tychmanska A (2021) The OECD as the future international tax organization: an inevitable course of events? Intertax 49(8/9)
Webber C, Wildavsky A (1986) A history of taxation and expenditure in the western world, Simon and Schuster edition

Chapter 6
Technology of International Taxation

Contents

6.1 The Curiosity of Human Beings

Technology is a matter of curiosity; the word comes from the Greek words "techne", meaning art, craft, or skill, and "logos", meaning word, discourse, or reasoning, and it is profoundly reshaping the landscape of international taxation, introducing both opportunities and challenges for governments, businesses, and Tax Authorities around the world. Rapid advancements in digital technologies have created new economic models, altered traditional business practices and presented complex issues for tax systems designed for a pre-digital era. Many scandals in international taxation (LGT, UBS, HSBC, Lux Leaks, Panama Papers and Paradise Papers) are linked to the transformation, from paper to digital, of data archives that were downloaded and made public upon compensation, and one could say that technology has begun its dominance when the change in the tools brought about the change in the purpose, as the Italian phylosopher Emanuele Severino dramatically warns in his essay "Capitalismo senza futuro" (Capitalism without future). Today, technology means transparency.

The rise of the digital economy has fundamentally changed how businesses operate and generate profits from local to global. Multinational companies like Apple, Google, Amazon, Meta (Facebook), Netflix, and Spotify leverage digital platforms to reach global markets, often generating significant revenues in jurisdictions where they may not have a physical presence. This has created a challenge for traditional tax systems, which typically rely on physical presence and tangible assets to

G. Marino, *The Dark Side of International Tax Law*,
https://doi.org/10.1007/978-3-032-08159-9_6

determine tax liability. Nobody should be worried insofar as food could not be downloaded; however, this is not true for governments that see taxpayers disappearing with a tremendous loss in revenue.

First, the allocation of profits in the digital economy is challenging because traditional tax rules were designed for "brick-and-mortar" businesses with physical presence. Companies can generate substantial revenue from users in a country without having a significant physical footprint, leading to debates on how to allocate taxing rights. Activities that require only a screen, a smartphone and a modem can be located anywhere. This makes it harder for a country to tax businesses much more heavily than its competitors.

Second, globalization makes it hard to decide where a company should pay tax, regardless of where it is based. Multinational companies design their products in one country, manufacture them in another, and sell them in a third country. This gives them plenty of scope to reduce tax obligations by shifting operations around or by crafty transfer pricing. Specifically, digital businesses often use strategies to minimize their tax liabilities by shifting profits to low-tax jurisdictions. This erosion of the tax base has prompted many countries to seek ways to capture a fair share of taxes from digital companies.

Third, in response to the challenges posed by digitalization, the Organisation for Economic Co-operation and Development's (OECD) Base Erosion and Profit Shifting (BEPS 1.0) project has become a cornerstone of international tax reform. Launched in 2013, the BEPS 1.0 project aims to address tax avoidance strategies that exploit gaps and mismatches in tax rules.

The BEPS Action Plan includes 15 actions designed to prevent base erosion and profit shifting. Key actions include measures to tackle harmful tax practices, improve transparency, and enhance the effectiveness of international tax rules. BEPS 1.0 has not been enough to calm down the base erosion and profit shifting, and the OECD, together with the G20, had to come back on digital taxation with BEPS 2.0, leading to proposals for new rules that would allocate more taxing rights to market jurisdictions where users and consumers are located. This is intended to address the issues of profit shifting and ensure that digital businesses contribute fairly to tax revenues. Unfortunately, the success of this new international tax regime is yet to be achieved.

Furthermore, technological advancements in automation and data analytics are transforming how Tax Authorities operate and enforce tax laws. These technologies enable more efficient processing and analysis of vast amounts of data, thereby improving tax compliance and enforcement. Tax Authorities are increasingly using data analytics to detect patterns of non-compliance, identify potential tax evasion, and improve audit effectiveness. Automated systems can analyse transaction data in real time, providing insights that were previously difficult to obtain. Many countries are implementing electronic invoicing and digital reporting requirements to streamline Tax Administration and enhance accuracy. This shift to digital reporting helps reduce errors, combat fraud, and improve the efficiency of tax collection.

The rise in cryptocurrencies and blockchain technology presents new challenges and opportunities for international taxation. Cryptocurrencies like Bitcoin and

Ethereum are decentralized and operate across borders, complicating tax enforcement and regulation. Determining how to tax cryptocurrencies involves addressing issues related to classification (e.g. whether they are treated as currencies, commodities, or assets), valuation, and reporting. Many jurisdictions are still developing frameworks to effectively tax and regulate digital assets. Blockchain technology has potential applications in improving tax compliance and transparency. By providing a tamper-proof ledger for transactions, the blockchain can enhance traceability and reduce opportunities for tax evasion.

In conclusion, the global nature of technology-driven businesses requires international cooperation to address tax challenges. Efforts to create a cohesive global tax framework face several hurdles, including differing national interests and the complexity of aligning diverse tax systems. Achieving international consensus on new tax rules for the digital economy is challenging due to differing national priorities and economic interests. The OECD's Inclusive Framework on BEPS 1.0 and BEPS 2.0 aims to bring countries together to develop unified approaches, but progress has been slow and complex.

References

Baumann-Larse S, Giannelli A (2020) The latest generation of tax functions and the role of technology. Bull Int Tax 10
Severino E (2012), Capitalismo senza futuro, Rizzoli
Streicher B (ed) (2023) Tax and technology, Series on international tax law. Linde Verlag
van Brederode RF (2012) Science technology and taxation, series on international taxation. Wolters Kluwer
Weber D (ed) (2023) The implications of online platforms and technology on taxation, GREIT Series. IBFD
Zackrisson M, Bakker A, Hagelin J (2020) AI and tax administrations: a good match. Bull Int Tax 10

Chapter 7
Jurisdiction to Tax Criteria in a Worldwide System

Contents

7.1 Preliminary Remarks: The Material Connections

This chapter focuses on who has the right to tax. In international law, there are two generally accepted connecting criteria for the determination of jurisdiction: either the citizenship of individuals and nationality of corporations, or territoriality. A country has jurisdiction over its citizens regardless of where they are located because they have a link of political allegiance to it, while it also has jurisdiction over persons or things within its territory.

In international taxation, political allegiance has been overridden by the economic allegiance that reminds us more of the cost theory (where taxes are paid to cover the costs of goods and services provided by the local government) than the redistributive theory (where resources are allocated in the social community regardless of the effective public economic benefits to the single taxpayer). Almost a paradox, considering that the redistributive theory is related to worldwide tax systems, while the cost theory is related to territorial tax systems.

The United States is the sole jurisdiction that makes use of political allegiance as the connecting criterion; this choice goes back to the American Civil War and is unlikely to be changed, although it causes many practical problems at the international level.

G. Marino, *The Dark Side of International Tax Law*,
https://doi.org/10.1007/978-3-032-08159-9_7

International tax law has translated economic allegiance into the principle of residence, which is useful both to the State of residence, asking for worldwide taxation, as well as to the State of source, asking for territorial taxation. Many States of the international community are worldwide and territorial, asking at the same time of their resident taxpayers to pay taxes on their worldwide income and of non-resident taxpayers to pay taxes on income produced within their own territories.

Worldwide versus territorial taxation is not only a matter of income taxes but could likely be a matter of the tax system. For example, as far as Italian succession and gift tax are concerned, if the de cuius or donor is resident in Italy, the heirs or the donees, wherever they are resident in the world, must pay the tax on any transferred asset wherever it is located in the world, while if the de cuius or donor is non-resident in Italy, the heirs or the donees, wherever they are resident in the world, must pay the tax only on the transferred assets that are located in Italy.

7.2 The Tax Residence of Individuals

Each single country has its own domestic definition of tax residence of individuals for the determination of its tax jurisdiction, although the connecting criteria are almost the same: 1) permanent home available, 2) centre of vital interests and 3) habitual abode. However, the connecting criteria are not sufficient to determine the tax residence of an individual, since the definition of tax residence is generally also based on counting days of physical presence in the given country. Hence, only an individual who has either a permanent home available, the centre of vital interests or a habitual abode for the greater part of the taxable period (i.e. more than 183 days) is a resident taxpayer of that country.

As regards the concept of home, it should be observed that any form of home may be considered (house or apartment belonging to or rented by the individual, rented furnished room). But the permanence of the home is essential; this means that the individual has arranged to always have the dwelling available to him continuously and not occasionally for the purpose of a stay which, owing to the reasons for it, is necessarily of short duration (travel for pleasure, business travel, educational travel, attending a course at a school, etc.).

As far as the centre of vital interests is concerned, that is related to the personal and economic relations of the individual, and where they are closer. In many civil-law countries, this is better known as ‘domicile’. Thus, regard must be given to his family and social relations, his occupations, his political, cultural, or other activities, his place of business, the place from which he administers his property, etc.

Last but not least, the habitual abode is a connecting criterion lighter than the permanent home available but nevertheless useful to determine whether an individual is satisfying the minimum threshold of living in each country. A remote, but interesting, interpretation of habitual abode is whether “habitual” might be “solo animo”, in other words, only with the proved intention of the taxpayer in the place to be, and not with his physical connection.

It is likely possible that due to ever-increasing international mobility, an individual is deemed to be a resident taxpayer in two countries at the same time because of their domestic tax legislations, with the consequence of double worldwide taxation. Technology, through devices, may certainly help Tax Administrations in the location of individuals, and where that is not enough, the Model Tax Convention (MTC), established by the Organisation for Economic Co-operation and Development (OECD) for the elimination of double taxation on income and capital, provides for a solution that is based on the application of the so-called "tie-breaker rules".

Article 4 of the MTC states that if an individual is deemed to be resident in both Contracting States by virtue of their domestic legislation, preference must be given to the State where the individual has their permanent home available. If the individual has a permanent home available in both Contracting States, then preference must be given to the State where the individual has his centre of vital interests. In cases where residence cannot be determined by reference to this last rule, Article 2, paragraph 2 of the MTC provides, as subsidiary criteria, first, habitual abode, and then citizenship. If the individual is a citizen of both States or neither of them, the question shall be solved by mutual agreement between the States concerned, according to the procedure laid down in Article 25 of the MTC.

There are many cases dealing with the double tax residence of individuals; the most interesting are those where residence is involved in an offshore jurisdiction where there are no income taxes or they are very low. In Europe, these jurisdictions happen to be Monaco and Switzerland, and case law generally involves artists, sportsmen and high net worth individuals moving there to take shelter from heavy worldwide taxation in their country of origin.

2.1. The opera singer Luciano Pavarotti, for example, decided to move his tax residence from Italy to Monaco. He rented an apartment there but still had an apartment available in Modena. At the same time, he got separated from his wife, so he assumed that his centre of vital interests was no longer in Italy. However, the Italian Tax Administration started to collect much information and documents (in a Jurassic era from the technological point of view) to obtain evidence of the presence of Pavarotti in Italy, and they questioned that because of (i) the income produced in Italy, (ii) the wealth owned in Italy and (iii) the consumption produced in Italy, Pavarotti was not resident in Monaco but resident in Italy. Pavarotti replied that he had his permanent home available in Monaco, but the Tax Administration reacted, saying that he was living in 150 square metres with a part-time housekeeper; meanwhile, his real estate in Modena was much bigger, with a full-time family of housekeepers sending their children to school in Modena.

As far as his centre of vital interests (domicile) was concerned, notwithstanding that Pavarotti got separated from his wife, it came out that he had a lover in Bologna named Nicoletta Mantovani, so the Tax Administration replied that the centre of vital interests was in Bologna (neither in Monaco nor in Modena).

The Tax Court of Appeal of Bologna (Div. 19, n. 16/19/00 of 27 March 2000) gave the right to the Tax Administration; however, Pavarotti lost the battle but won the war because he never disclosed his worldwide economic interests. At that time, the Italian Tax Administration was not in a position to collect information from third countries on how much money he was earning from his concerts. If he had disclosed his financial information, he could have won the battle but lost the war if the judge declared him a tax resident in Italy. The Tax Administration would have taken all the information on his worldwide income and taxed it in Italy. Therefore, he has been very bright, not showing the entire scenario of his economic interests. When he died, it came out that because of the fight, he put all his financial assets into a trust, nominating as the beneficiary of the trust his lover, Nicoletta Mantovani. The case never went up to the Supreme Court, but it stopped at the Court of Appeal. Pavarotti paid the money for the income he produced in Italy, and that was it. In conclusion, *Nessun dorma!*

2.2. As a matter of tax competition, each country tries to attract rich people from other countries by offering an appealing tax product to the individual taxpayer. There is indeed a sort of international tax supermarket where the taxpayer does their shopping by deciding which product to purchase. Individuals are moving all around the world. You must run away from the country. It is the only solution, because if you move, after some years, you will reach the condition to get a tax advantage elsewhere. A sort of 'tax me if you can'.

The leading country in the international tax supermarket was the United Kingdom because of its legal background since 1799 to manage at best the relationship with people coming from the colonies of its empire. Under UK tax legislation, if an individual did not have a British passport, he could be considered as a "resident not domiciled", meaning that he was resident because of his permanent home available in the UK but not domiciled because of his origins (place of birth, citizenship, language, family of origin, etc.). From a British income tax perspective, a resident who was not domiciled was only taxed on income produced within the UK, while his foreign income was taxed in the UK only if it was remitted into a British bank account. That was also fair from the standpoint of the politics of international taxation; there was no need to let the resident not domiciled pay worldwide so far, and the UK did not offer him any financial and political protection outside its own territory.

Unfortunately, the UK government has abolished the long-standing non-domiciled tax regime, starting from 6 April 2025. This regime allowed wealthy foreign nationals living in the UK—but officially "domiciled" elsewhere—to avoid paying UK tax on their foreign income and capital gains if they did not bring that money into the UK (known as the remittance basis). For years, this policy has made the UK, particularly London, a magnet for global elites. Billionaires, entrepreneurs, and international professionals took advantage of this rule to live luxuriously in the UK while shielding substantial offshore wealth from the Her Majesty's Revenue and Customs (HMRC). But that's all about to change.

For one country leaving the international tax supermarket, another one enters. Since 2017, Italy has introduced a favourable tax regime for high-net-worth individuals (HNWIs) who have spent 9 out of 10 years abroad. If they move their residence to the country, they can pay for 15 years a minimum lump sum substituting the income and inheritance taxation on their foreign assets. The tax product was launched after Brexit to attract wealthy people spending money in Italy while keeping their investments out of the country.

The difference from the US is clear. The US exercises its power to tax worldwide on the basis of citizenship, regardless of the tax residence of its citizens, and protects them with the Navy, the Army and the Air Force all over the world. The mechanism to catch the movements of US citizens all over the world is made through a program called the Foreign Account Tax Compliance Act (FATCA), through which the US requires all other countries to ask their local banks to reveal the identity of any American bank account holder to the Internal Revenue Service to apply worldwide taxation. Very much different from the UK, which did not give protection worldwide and did not ask for money worldwide from its residents not domiciled.

However, the Trump Administration has announced a "gold visa" programme offering the status of resident not domiciled to those foreign individuals who are able to invest at least 5 million dollars in the US, launching the US tax system as the priority for high-net-worth individuals who want to feel safe from worldwide income taxation.

7.3 The Tax Residence of Corporations

God created a man in his image and likeness, and the man created the corporation, giving it a legal personality to not be outdone. Nature imposes nine months on a woman to create a baby, while a corporation can be created in a few minutes without pain. A corporation is a legal entity between shareholders and a group of individuals running a business activity on their behalf. The number of shareholders, the kind of business (whether industry, banking, finance, insurance, high-tech or agriculture) and the size of its organization determine whether the interposition is real or fictitious. If it is real, the corporation shall be subject to tax; if it is fictitious, shareholders shall be deemed to bring the tax consequences as if the company were not existing. World revenue today depends more on corporations (namely, on individuals as employees of the organization) than on individuals as self-employed; they represent so many people and move so many interests that corporate taxation is a natural consequence. The corporation does not eat at the restaurant, does not go to jail, but certainly pays all the bills.

Taxes on corporations are (i) desirable to collect public revenue in ways that would improve the economic well-being, not harm the economic well-being, or impose costs on those beyond the political pale; (ii) necessary as an essential component of any adequate system of personal taxation and (iii) convenient since they are imposed at a "conduit" level that makes it virtually inconceivable not to do so.

Like individual taxpayers, corporations shall be subject to worldwide or territorial taxation depending on whether they are resident or not resident in a State, and the connecting criteria used to link them to a territory look like those used for individuals. For example, the place of incorporation, being the place where the corporation was born, can look like either citizenship or the centre of vital interests, that is, the domicile of an individual. The place of effective management is where managers make decisions and employees run the business, which looks like a permanent home available of an individual. These are the main criteria in international tax law to determine which is the country of residence and which is the country of source, together with the temporal criterion of the greater part of the taxable period.

There are countries that use a combination of criteria in their domestic tax law and countries that use just one of the criteria. The latter is the case of the US tax system, making only reference to the place of incorporation to determine the residence and nationality of a corporation, and the case of Ireland, making only reference to the place of effective management to determine whether a corporation is an Irish tax resident. This means that if you set up a corporation in Ireland that is managed in the US, you will end up with a vehicle resident nowhere, as the tech giants were before the Apple case.

3.1. When a corporation is considered a tax resident under the domestic tax legislation of more than one country, and there are tax treaties following the OECD MTC to regulate among them the elimination of double taxation, Article 4, paragraph 3, used to provide that corporations are deemed to be a resident only of the State in which their place of effective management (POEM) is situated for the greater part of the taxable period.

It is not easy to determine the place of effective management since there are many levels within the decision-making process, and each individual matching the level may well be resident in the territory of a single State that may have the right to claim that a place of effective management is under its jurisdiction. The chief executive officer (CEO) is the most powerful manager, together with the chief operating officer (COO) and chief financial officer (CFO), and they may effectively work from anywhere in the world. However, they must report their decisions to the board of directors that has appointed them in their roles, and the board of directors may well be spread all over the world and connected in chat. Finally, the board of directors of a corporation is appointed by the shareholders' meeting, and if there is a controlling shareholder, it is important to verify where that shareholder (individual or corporation) is resident (in this case, the best definition is the place of effective management and control).

So far, single individuals within the chain of the decision-making process are resident in many jurisdictions, and the place where the execution of their decisions is handled could be an alternative perspective to look at the place of effective management. The place of execution looks like the place of business activity, and there might be cases where the two places match each other. This is the reason why, in the Observations on the Commentary at Article 4 of the MTC, Italy holds the view that the place where the main and substantial activity of the entity is carried on is also to be considered when determining the place of effective management of a person other than an individual.

3.2. It is worth mentioning the oldest case of corporate tax residence and the most glamorous, at least from the Italian point of view. The first is the "De Beers Consolidated Mines, Limited, Appellants; Howe (Surveyors of Taxes), Respondent" of the UK Court of Appeal, 17 April 1905, n. 2K.B. 612. De Beers is a multinational corporation dealing with diamonds (one of the largest diamond corporations all over the world). De Beers was incorporated in South Africa, but it had its place of effective management in London, where it decided how many diamonds to source from Africa and sell in London. The board of directors of the company was composed of 16 directors: 4 residents in the UK and 12 residents in South Africa. There were also three life governors. Board meetings were held in South Africa and London. The 12 directors in South Africa needed to ask for authorization from the directors in London to take their ordinary decisions. Extraordinary decisions (about how many diamonds to put on the market every year) were taken in London. The UK Inland Revenue claimed that the POEM of De Beers was in the UK and not in South Africa, although the corporation was incorporated there, and the judge confirmed that, for tax purposes, the place of effective management is more important than the place of incorporation. In conclusion, taxes are forever, like diamonds!

The most glamorous is the Italian Dolce & Gabbana case (Fig. 7.1). The two stylists decided to structure their businesses in an international way. The Italian D&G company set up a D&G company in Luxembourg. D&G Luxembourg set up a D&G company in Luxembourg (GADO) and another one in Italy. They sold to this latter company the exclusive use of their name.

GADO gave a licence to D&G, and in exchange for this licence, D&G Italy paid royalties to GADO. The royalty was a cost for the D&G, not a profit. The more D&G sold products, the higher the royalty paid to GADO. On the other hand, GADO, being a resident in Luxembourg, the place of incorporation, and because of its place of effective management, was paying taxes on worldwide income in Luxembourg, so all the royalties received based on the licence of the trademark all over the world were taxed in Luxembourg. But Luxembourg is a small country, and

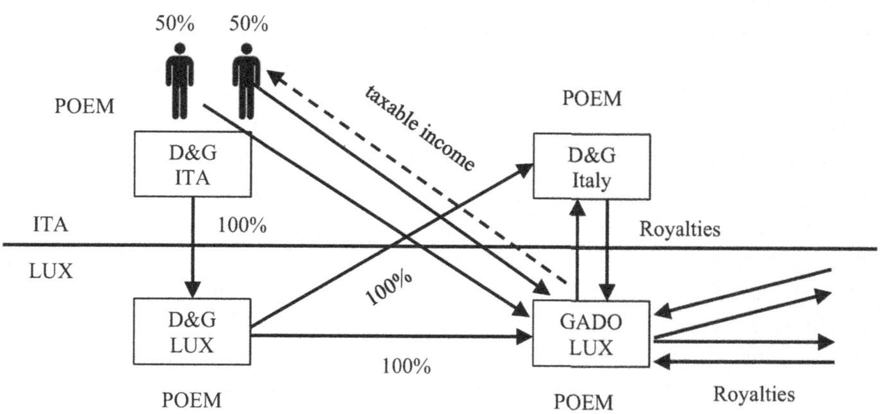

Fig. 7.1 The reverse corporate tax residence

it offered large discounts in taxation, and this was the reason why GADO, as well as D&G Luxembourg, were incorporated in Luxembourg, having their POEM in Luxembourg because all the royalties (being the core of D&G business profit) were taxed in Luxembourg and not in Italy. On the other hand, the royalties in Italy were a cost, so the revenue in Italy was decreasing, and the shift of the trademark was shifted for a very low value.

The Italian Tax Police (Guardia di Finanza) inspected and discovered that the directors of D&G Italy were instructing their companies in Luxembourg on how to do their business and at what price to set up the royalties, so their decisions were taken according to what was decided in Italy. The Tax Police concluded for an "esterovestizione" (reverse corporate tax residence or sham residence) and that the POEM of GADO was not in Luxembourg, but it was at the place where D&G Italy was run. But if the POEM of GADO is for more than 183 days in Italy, the conclusion is that GADO, even if it has been incorporated in Luxembourg, is resident in Italy: this happened because the decisions were taken by directors of D&G Italy. So GADO has no autonomy in doing its business (as in the De Beers case: directors in London were making strategic decisions). Here, the Italian directors were taking the strategic decisions to be only executed by the Luxembourg directors, and if these strategic decisions were taken for more than 183 days in the Italian territory, that means that GADO is not resident in Luxembourg but in Italy. Therefore, all royalties received by the GADO should be taxed as corporate taxes in Italy on a worldwide basis, not in Luxembourg. But what about the Luxembourg Authorities? They may say that GADO is resident in Luxembourg because of the place of incorporation and because decisions taken by directors in Luxembourg, even if those decisions were received by Italian directors, were signed in Luxembourg, so the Luxembourg Authority could say that GADO was resident in its territory. This is a case of conflict of residence: there is a dual residence company with international double taxation because it has been taxed in Luxembourg, but Italy is asking for taxes.

But to be concrete, who is entitled to say where the POEM is? The MTC says nothing about it, and in theory, both Contracting States should sit around a table and decide where the POEM is. The reality is that any taxpayer suffering double taxation needs to ask the judge of the jurisdiction claiming the tax residence for the application of the tie-breaker rules.

In the D&G case, the Tax Police said that because of the very low sales of the trademark, this is a tax crime, so they transferred the case to the criminal prosecutor, switching the claim into a criminal tax case and an administrative tax case. The criminal prosecutor also prosecuted the tax advisor because they realised that D&G were just tailors; they could not manage alone the creation of such an international corporate tax scheme. The two litigations went further, and Dolce and Gabbana won in both cases: 1) on the criminal side: the Supreme Court (Cass. Pen. Sez. III, 30 October 2015, n. 43809) stated there was no tax fraud but tax avoidance, and 2) on the administrative side: the Supreme Court (Cass. Civ. Sez. V, 21 December 2018, n. 33234) stated that if GADO is incorporated in Luxembourg and if this company has directors taking decisions, there was indeed a purpose for being present with its directors in Luxembourg. This interpretation is enough to say that POEM was indeed in Luxembourg and not in Italy. Since they also won the case on the administrative side, the Revenue had to give the money back.

3.3. If a corporation has been incorporated in Ireland and has its place of effective management and control in the US, what is the conclusion? That corporation is a resident nowhere; it is a resident alien corporation. This is a case of international double non-taxation rather than a case of international double taxation. Apple, as well as many other tech giants, used to be structured as a group in a layout called by the nickname "Double Irish with a Dutch sandwich", having Irish resident corporations for US tax purposes and US resident corporations for Irish (European) tax purposes. This is the other edge of the international tax law philosophy. This case brought problems to international revenue for the entire world.

There were two Irish companies (Fig. 7.2): Apple Operations Europe and Apple Sales International. In between them, there is a Dutch company, Apple Netherlands. The Dutch are very clever in finance; a small country, they are the best. They always remain in between. Apple Sales International was incorporated in Ireland; POEM was also in Ireland but was granted a tax ruling on transfer pricing that resulted in zero income tax in the country. Apple Operations Europe had its place of incorporation in Ireland but its POEM in Bermuda. So, if the only criterion is POEM, they were not resident in the US, and they could not be taxed in the US.

Apple used to sell intellectual property for a reasonable amount of money to Apple Operations Europe (the same concept as D&G selling trademarks to GADO) while research and development was conducted in Cupertino (US). So, Apple Operations Europe was buying intellectual property and paying something back, and once it had intellectual property, it could license it. It licensed intellectual property to the Netherlands. Apple Netherlands sublicensed the Intellectual Property (IP) to Apple Sales International (the distributor), which, based on the sublicence of

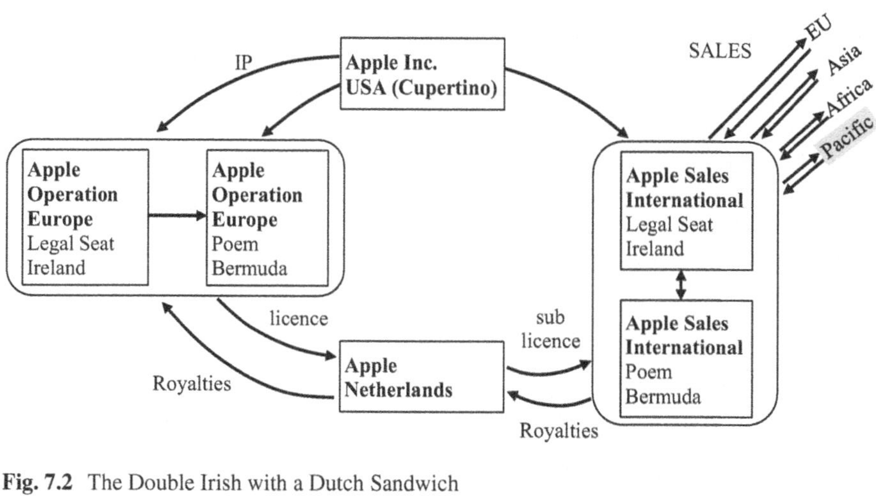

Fig. 7.2 The Double Irish with a Dutch Sandwich

the IP having the iPhone, was then selling iPhones all over the world, and it could pay back royalties because of the sales of the iPhones. Based on this, Apple Sales International had to pay a royalty to the Netherlands, and the Netherlands had to pay a royalty to Apple Operations Europe. Why is intermediation in the Netherlands? It was important to reduce taxes on royalties as much as possible (the Netherlands has a large tax treaty network, having zero taxation on royalties). In the end, Apple has accumulated profits from all sales around the world by leaving these profits in the cloud in both its structures. So, Apple did not pay taxes everywhere.

In the stock exchange of New York, the price of the shares was always going up for the pleasure of its shareholders and the US Revenue for the related capital gains tax in the case of sale. Apple in Europe was not paying a single euro of tax, and this violated the European principle of a ban on state aid, as stated in the European Court of Justice (ECJ) decision on 10 September 2024, C-465/20 P.

3.4. The international debate on the tax residence of companies is driven by the consideration that digitalization of the global economy has allowed for the creation of many large companies that are not resident in any jurisdiction. As such, they not only avoid the problem of double taxation but also benefit from situations of double non-taxation.

Action 6 of the Base Erosion and Profit Shifting (BEPS) project recommended countering these aggressive tax planning mechanisms through the modification of the "tie-breaker rules" provided by Article 4 of the OECD Model Tax Convention. Before the changes introduced by Action 6 of the BEPS Project, Article 4, paragraph 3 of the OECD Model Convention referred to the State in which the POEM of the enterprise was located—that is, the place where the most important decisions regarding the company's management were made. Following the changes, however, the new text of Article 4, paragraph 3, adopts a "case-by-case" approach to resolve "residence conflicts" concerning companies, where it is up to the States to initiate "Mutual Agreement Procedures" (MAP) under Article 25 of the OECD Model to determine which of the two countries is entitled to consider the company resident in its territory under the treaty. The provision also identifies the criteria by which the Authorities of the Contracting States can reach an agreement on the residence of companies, namely, the "place of effective management", the place of incorporation, or other factors deemed relevant for this purpose. The first two criteria are precisely those that have created the conditions for companies to have dual residency under the domestic laws of different States or to have none, allowing them to perpetrate tax abuses.

Although the criteria outlined in the provision were already used in international tax law, the fact that States are allowed to consider other factors as well as determine the tax residence of companies could lead to discretionary decisions and, in the worst-case scenario, difficulties in reaching an agreement. This latter eventuality could arise if each State intends to apply the criterion it considers most suitable to ensure that the company is a tax resident in its territory, with the aim of securing its taxation. The difficulties described in reaching an agreement on the residences of companies certainly had a negative impact on the latter. Indeed, in the absence of an agreement, the provision stipulates that treaty benefits would be denied to the company. In this way, the OECD Model Tax Convention effectively discourages companies from engaging in tax planning based on dual tax residence, as a challenge by States would suspend the application of treaty benefits. In short, no Dutch sandwiches exist in Irish Bun.

It may be precisely for this reason that, despite the new measures specifically aimed at combating treaty abuse through tax strategies based on dual (non) residence, few countries in the international community have adopted this approach under the OECD Multilateral Convention. Most countries today still prefer to rely on the "place of effective management" criterion to resolve residence conflicts, even though, in practice, it has not proven capable in the past of combating various forms of international tax avoidance.

At the supranational level of the European Union, on the other hand, the tax discipline of the "esterovestizione" (reverse corporate tax residence or sham residence) would impose a restriction on the freedom of establishment, as it would hinder companies resident in one Member State from establishing subsidiaries in another Member State to avoid the presumption under examination. In this regard, it should be remembered that restrictions on the fundamental freedoms underlying European Union (EU) principles are justified only when they aim to protect a legitimate interest, provided they are not disproportionate to their purpose (ECJ Cadbury Schweppes Decision, 12 September 2006, No. C-196/04).

References

Avi-Yonah RS (2014) And yet it moves: taxation and labor mobility in the twenty-first century. Tax Law Rev 67:2

Clifton Fleming Jr J, Peroni RJ, Shay SF (2016) Defending worldwide taxation with a shareholder-based definition of corporate residence. BYU Law Rev 1681

Lipniewicz R (2020) Place of effective management in the digital economy. Intertax 48(6/7)

Mason R (2016) Citizenship taxation. South Calif Law Rev 89:169

Sanchirico CW (2015) As American as Apple Inc.: international tax and ownership nationality. Tax Law Rev 68:207

Chapter 8
Jurisdiction to Tax Criteria in a Territorial System

Contents

8.1 Preliminary Remarks: Active Versus Passive Income

As far as the nexus for territorial taxation is concerned, the State of source may easily find its jurisdiction to tax when the ability to pay consists of wealth and consumption, while when income is considered, it is necessary to divide its passive from its active perspective.

Passive income is the income generated from capital investments, and it can be divided into three categories of return: 1) dividends from shares and the like; 2) interest from bonds and the like and 3) capital gains from the sale of shares or from the sale of bonds and the like. The mix is also known as income from the portfolio or, better, passive income, since the taxpayers neither control the source nor add personal energy to determine its production.

On the other hand, active income is (i) the income generated from employment performed under the direction of somebody else (i.e. wages and salaries), (ii) the income from self-employment or, last but not least, (iii) the income from business when a taxpayer entrepreneur combines labour and capital to set up his own organization to carry on an activity. Income from real estate is also generally deemed to be

G. Marino, *The Dark Side of International Tax Law*,
https://doi.org/10.1007/978-3-032-08159-9_8

active income rather than passive income, since there is always an activity behind rental income.

The Report on Double Taxation of 1923 provides the "first bite to the apple" rule, under which, between the residence and source, the rights of the source country must prevail because the income arises within the source country, and the residence country cannot prevent the source country from having the jurisdiction to tax that income, whether passive or active. However, specific (formal) rules are necessary to understand when passive income is linked to the country of source, while specific (substantive) rules are necessary to understand when active income is linked to the country of source.

1.1. The formal rules are based on the residence of a person, whether natural or legal, other than the taxpayer: 1) in the case of dividends, it comes to evidence the residence of the distributing company; and 2) in the case of interests, it comes to evidence the residence of the payor. The latter rule is under pressure because of the globalization of the economy. For example, imagine an individual taxpayer who is a resident of country A and wants to buy real estate in country B. He asks for a mortgage loan from a bank in country B. He opens a bank account in the same bank to transfer the money to complete the acquisition and pays back the mortgage loan. Notwithstanding that the transaction is entirely executed in country B, the bank is producing passive income in country A, where it has to pay income tax since the payor is resident there.

Last but not least, the residence of the taxpayer also becomes relevant in capital gains taxation since the company whose shares are sold is not by itself involved in the transaction; hence, its residence is not relevant.

Also, this latter rule may lead to some distortions since the State of source, being the State where the company whose shares are sold is resident, does not have jurisdiction to tax, notwithstanding the fact that the value of the company is reflected in the value of the shares, which only the State of residence of the seller is entitled to tax.

The Vodafone case confirmed that this is the rule, at least in the presence of a bilateral tax treaty following the Organisation for Economic Co-operation and Development (OECD) Model Tax Convention (MTC). Vodafone wanted to enter the Indian market and acquired the shares of an Indian resident company dealing with the telecommunications business. A Dutch company of the Vodafone group acquired shares from the seller, which was a company resident in Mauritius. Under the tax treaty between India and Mauritius, the capital gains realized from the sale of shares were only taxable in Mauritius, being the seller's State of residence. However, the Indian Tax Administration challenged the transaction by claiming that the scheme was abusive since the selling company was avoiding paying tax in the State of source because of the tax treaty and asked the new shareholder of the Indian company, Vodafone Nederland, to pay the capital gains tax; otherwise, the shares could not be used to exercise its voting rights. Vodafone could then ask for the money back from the seller, but that would have been a private issue. The case has been discussed at all levels of the international community, and the Indian Supreme Court

(Decision 20 January 2012, n. 2012[6] SCC 613), in the end, rejected the claim of the Revenue and restored the international principle of jurisdiction to tax.

1.2. The substantive rules for the determination of the jurisdiction to tax depend on the kind of income: 1) in the case of wages and salaries, as well as in the case of self-employment, the place where the work is performed must be verified; 2) in the case of business income, the place where the company is located as a permanent establishment must be looked at and last but not the least; 3) in case of real estate income, it is relatively easy to imagine that jurisdiction to tax is with the State where the real estate is located.

1.3. Finally, there is a kind of income that is the main driver of the digital economy, whose nature, passive or active, is difficult to ascertain, and the jurisdiction to tax is consequently in trouble, that is, royalty income derived from the exploitation of a trademark or patent right.

The creation of an intangible asset is certainly a matter of activity, and substantive rules should be applied to determine the State of the source; however, the exploitation of an intangible asset is purely passive, and only formal rules can determine the State of the source. Nowadays, the value of a product is more in its technology than in its materiality, and this should mean that its acquisition price should reflect a portion of active income (subject to substantive rules) and a portion of passive income (subject to formal rules).

There are many cases dealing with the difficulty of framing the nature of royalty income from the perspective of the jurisdiction to tax. For example, in the *Korfund case* (Korfund Co. v. Commissioner of Internal Revenue; 1. T.C. 1180 (1943)), a German resident company was receiving money from a US corporation in order not to compete in the US market. Under substantive rules, the jurisdiction to tax should have been with the US because the market involved for the non-competition was the US, while under formal rules, it should have been the residence of the recipient, so Germany should have been entitled to tax. The case was in favour of Germany as the country of residence.

In the *Boulez case* (Boulez v. Commissioner 76 T.C. 209 (1981)), a German resident musician went to the US for an orchestra performance. Since the service was performed in the US, the profit of this self-employment income should have been taxed in the US. After the performance, the producer suggested that the musician record the performance and make a disc to be sold all over the world. Indeed, he was getting a royalty, a percentage, for the sale of the product of this recording; he was getting a royalty even if the sales were all over the world. So, the Internal Revenue Service (IRS), which was already receiving taxation on the performance of the orchestra, started to ask the musician for taxes on the royalties for the sales realized in the rest of the world because of the recording that was originally made in the US and then sold through the discs all over the world. At the same time, Germany was asking for taxation of royalties because the royalty is the passive income realized from the exploitation of patent rights, so it was a sort of passive income, and the patent right comes from the performance. The double taxation was solved by Germany granting credit for taxes paid in the US.

Finally, the Nobel Prize winner for chemistry, Paul Karrer, was a resident in Switzerland and was conducting research for a Swiss pharma corporation to develop some medical products. The payment for the research was a percentage of the sales made by the Swiss corporation in the US market. The IRS argued that this compensation was a royalty sourced to the US, but Karrer argued successfully that his contract was for services performed in Switzerland, having nothing to do with the US (Karrer v. United States, US Court of Claims, 8 May 1957).

A modern perspective on royalty for difficulties in determining jurisdiction to tax has to do with influencers. Their presence in a restaurant, the clothes they wear, or their daily life choices may influence the behaviour of their followers. They could get the right to be paid by the restaurant, the fashion house or any other business, depending on the likes they get on Instagram or any other social network, which are then translated into money. Where is the income of an influencer produced? In the country of the source or in his country of residence? However, this does not exclude double taxation. Many influencers, because of the problem of double taxation, reside in countries where they are protected from international double taxation.

1.4. The problem of the source has to do with deductions. Between the country of residence and the country of source, it is not only a matter of allocation of profits and related taxation but also a matter of allocation of costs, because many incomes need costs to be produced; no costs, no income. What about the deductions of the costs to produce income? This is a problem of income taxation: if a State wants to tax income, then it must also recognize the costs related to the production of that income.

The issue at the international level is the recognition of costs in the same terms as the recognition of income allocation between the country of residence and the country of source. For example, if a taxpayer receives a loan from a bank to make a foreign investment and needs to pay interest, the interest payment to the bank must be deducted entirely in the country where the loan was concluded or in the country where the loan was used to make the investment. This is a problem with cost allocation between the country of residence and the country of source.

The future of jurisdiction to tax has to do with the digitalization and globalization of the economy. What if all the abovementioned rules disappear? There is no taxation, but Facebook, Apple, Amazon, Netflix and Google (FAANG) make lots of profits in the country of source, but the Revenue gets nothing. We need to go beyond the source and residence. We are talking about the taxation of a disappearing taxpayer; nevertheless, they make a lot of money, and the problem of the future is to catch that money.

8.2 How to Exercise Jurisdiction to Tax for Passive Income: The Withholding Tax System

Jurisdiction to tax means who has the right to exercise the taxing power between the State of residence and the State of source, while what to tax is a matter of distinguishing passive from active income. It is now time to understand how the State of the source may tax passive as well as active income.

As far as passive income is concerned, the only connection that the non-resident taxpayer has with the State of source is the payor of that income, nothing else. This means that requiring the non-resident taxpayer to file a tax return would be inefficient and disproportionate and would also imply recognizing personal expenses and expenses related to that passive income that the non-resident taxpayer has incurred somewhere else other than the State of source. It is much better to ask the resident payor to act as a withholding tax agent on behalf of the non-resident taxpayer and in the interest of the State of source revenue. To do so, taxation should be based on the gross income paid by the resident payor.

The withholding tax system is very old and was first used in the modern English income tax of 1862 under the name of a 'stoppage at source', much earlier than international taxation came into existence. Since the 1930s, non-resident taxpayers who receive passive income have been taxed on a gross basis by withholding, and this tax is a final tax with no deductions allowed, generally applied with a proportional rate that is lower than the progressive income tax rates. From the perspective of the State of residence that has the duty to eliminate double taxation for all its resident taxpayers, such withholding is treated, for the purpose of the foreign tax credit, as a tax imposed by the State of source "in lieu" of the income tax. This enables the withholding tax to be credited even though it is not an income tax since it does not allow for deductions.

The range of withholding tax rates may vary depending on whether the passive income is a dividend, an interest or a royalty and to what extent the State of source needs to attract investments in its territory—investments in equity, debt or intangible assets. The greater the need, the lower the tax rate shall be. Furthermore, the lower the withholding tax rate, the happier the State of residence is going to be since its foreign tax credit will not erode much domestic revenue. Tax competition always lags behind the international withholding tax system.

This is the reason why the OECD has tried to regulate the application of withholding taxes on passive income by introducing Articles 10 (dividends), 11 (interests) and 12 (royalties), remarking that its indication is a recommendation to level the playing field for the tax rates. Here is the assumption:

Article 10 – **Dividends**

1. Dividends paid by a company which is a resident of a Contracting State to a resident of the other Contracting State may be taxed in that other State.
2. However, such dividends may also be taxed in the Contracting State of which the company paying the dividends is a resident and according to the laws of that State, but if the beneficial owner of the dividends is a resident of the other Contracting State, the tax so

charged shall not exceed: a) 5 per cent of the gross amount of the dividends if the beneficial owner is a company (other than a partnership) which holds directly at least 25 per cent of the capital of the company paying the dividends; b) 15 per cent of the gross amount of the dividends in all other cases. The competent authorities of the Contracting States shall by mutual agreement settle the mode of application of these limitations. This paragraph shall not affect the taxation of the company in respect of the profits out of which the dividends are paid.

In conclusion, (i) the withholding tax shall not exceed 5% of the dividends if the beneficial owner is a company that holds at least 25% of the capital of the company paying the dividends and (ii) shall not exceed 15% of the dividends in all other cases.

Article 11 – **Interests**

1. Interest arising in a Contracting State and paid to a resident of the other Contracting State may be taxed in that other State.
2. However, such interest may also be taxed in the Contracting State in which it arises and according to the laws of that State, but if the beneficial owner of the interest is a resident of the other Contracting State, the tax charged shall not exceed 10 per cent of the gross amount of the interest. The competent authorities of the Contracting States shall by mutual agreement settle the mode of application of this limitation.

Article 12 – **Royalties**

Royalties arising in a Contracting State and beneficially owned by a resident of the other Contracting State shall be taxable only in that other State.

8.3 The Tax Obligations for Active and Passive Income

Once it is understood what and how the territorial system can tax, it must be understood how to apply tax obligations. The discussion must distinguish active income from passive income:

- Active Income: If active income is produced, an income tax return must be filed in the country where the income is sourced. For example, if an individual from the U.S. owns and rents real estate in Italy, he must file a tax return in Italy for that property. This process helps the Tax Administration in the source country identify who he is. Importantly, he does not pay taxes on gross income but on net income after expenses.
- Passive Income: If passive income is generated, the source country will not request the filing of a tax return as would be done with active income. Instead, the tax obligation will be satisfied by way of the withholding tax system, through which the source country collects taxes from the resident payor of the dividend, interest and royalties. This system does not apply to capital gains. Through withholding tax, a percentage of the income is taken at the source by the resident payor and remitted directly to the local Revenue.

3.1. The responsibility for withholding and remitting taxes lies with the payor company in its State of residence, which is also the State of source. This means that the Tax Administration does not pursue the non-resident taxpayer directly but rather collects the tax from the resident payor company. The withholding tax system is straightforward because it uses a flat percentage from 5% to 30% on average. In Italy, for example, it is 26%. However, this tax is applied to gross income and not to net income. If the tax were applied to net income, considering related expenses, it would lower the tax due. However, recognizing these expenses might result in a higher progressive tax rate (in Italy, up to 43%), while taxing gross income leads to a lower, flat rate of 5% to 26% because expenses are not recognized.

The withholding tax system is quite old. For example, regarding dividends, if Italy is the resident country and the U.S. is the source country (where the corporation paying the dividends is based), lowering the withholding tax can attract more foreign investment, while higher taxes might deter it. The U.S., confident in its strong economy, maintains a 30% withholding tax. However, countries seeking to attract more foreign investment may lower their withholding taxes through bilateral treaties.

It is essential to differentiate between domestic withholding tax and treaty withholding tax. First, the taxpayer and its advisors must check the domestic withholding tax and then determine if a tax treaty can reduce it. For example, the U.S. produces many patents and copyrights, so it is in its interest that dividends be taxed only in the country of residence, not in the source country. Countries may negotiate treaties to lower withholding taxes and attract more investments.

The lower the withholding tax, the more attractive it is for foreign investors. This brings tax competition among countries, and investors often engage in "treaty shopping" to benefit from the most favourable tax treaties. This happens when taxpayers have the ambition to trace the optimal tax route from State of residence A to the State of source B by placing corporations in intermediary jurisdictions with favourable tax treaty networks (like the Netherlands and Luxembourg) in terms of reduced withholding taxes on passive income. This is no different from international airports, which work as hubs for national flight companies. If you buy a ticket to fly from A to B via Amsterdam, London, or Dubai, you generally spend less money than flying directly.

For instance, an Italian investor might prefer to invest through the Netherlands Antilles to take advantage of the lower withholding taxes between the U.S. and the Netherlands Antilles. This practice aims to minimize withholding taxes, which is known as treaty shopping. However, this can lead to international double non-taxation, in which income is taxed very little or not at all.

This is the reason why the international community, following the US example of limitation of benefit (LOB) clauses under its tax treaties, has well established that the benefits of lower treaty withholding tax rates are only available to taxpayers who are the ultimate beneficial owners of passive income, and the payor has the duty, under its own responsibility, to verify whether the non-resident recipient respects that condition.

There are several interesting cases dealing with treaty shopping: 1) the SDI case (1996), 2) the Prevost case (2008), 3) the Indofood case (2006) and 4) the Danish cases (C-116/16, C-117/16). These cases aim to determine the "beneficial owner" of the income, which helps identify where the income should be taxed and which treaty should be applied. The Netherlands is often involved in treaty shopping due to its strong fiscal system, positioning itself as a central player in global financial flows despite its small economy. The revolution in the beneficial ownership definition shall be described in Chap. 14.

As far as active income is concerned, the way the State of source exercises its taxing power is through the request of filing a tax return to the non-resident taxpayer producing in the territory wages and salaries, self-employment income, business income or real estate income. In the case that non-resident taxpayers do not file a tax return, there is no way to escape the possibility that the State of source seizes their local assets.

International taxation is rapidly evolving, with technology helping countries identify beneficial owners of income. For example, the U.S. introduced the Foreign Account Tax Compliance Act (FATCA) to track U.S. citizens with foreign accounts. Banks worldwide have agreed to participate in FATCA, sharing information with the U.S. about their U.S. clients. This global push for transparency means that banking secrecy is diminishing, making it increasingly difficult for taxpayers to hide their income internationally.

8.4 The Future of the Withholding Tax Agent

The taxpayer may disappear, but the withholding tax agent can never disappear. It could be argued that the withholding tax agent is even more important than the taxpayer itself, since it is the subject having many times the tax duty on its shoulders on behalf of the taxpayer. The role of the tax agent is expanding more and more in the globalized economy, from the Common Reporting Standard (CRS) providing for automatic exchange of financial information between countries to the whistleblowing of potentially aggressive tax-planning arrangements spanning across more than one jurisdiction, the disclosure of which would bring additional positive results where that information was also exchanged among countries (that is the case of the European Directive on Administrative Cooperation [DAC] 6).

Airbnb Ireland has been involved in case law both in Europe (ECJ, 22 December 2022, C-83/2021) and in Italy (State Council, 24 October 2023, n. 9188) where it has been found obliged to collect the 21% tax substituting the individual income tax (Irpef) on the rental income derived from Italian real estate, intermediated by the company, on behalf of their owners.

References

de Mooij RA, Klemm AD, Perry VJ (2021) Corporate income taxes under pressure: why reform is needed and how it could be designed. International Monetary Fund

Haase F (2023) Withholding taxation in the EU, Elgar Tax Law and Practice Series
Helminen M (2020) Taxation of passive income. In: HJI Panayi C, Haslehner W, Traversa E (eds) Research handbook on EU taxation law. Edward Elgar
Shimizu M (2021) Effects of tax payment systems on tax compliance: comparing the withholding system with the tax declaration system. J Behav Econ Policy, Society for the Advancement of Behavioral Economics (SABE) 5(S2)

Chapter 9
Inbound Taxation

Contents

9.1 Preliminary Remarks: The Permanent Establishment

While passive income is taxed in the State of source by way of a withholding tax system, active income earned in the territory of the State of source is taxed by way of a tax return that the non-resident taxpayer has the duty to file. This involves (i) income from wages and salaries, (ii) income from self-employment, (iii) income from business activities carried on through permanent establishments, and (iv) income from real estate.

As far as business income is concerned, it is worth noting that the 1923 Report on Double Taxation was already providing that the minimum threshold to talk about business activity in the State of source was to have a permanent establishment there. If there is no permanent establishment in the State of source, it is impossible to talk about the business activity of a non-resident taxpayer there.

At that time, the kind of minimum presence was represented by an industrial factory, a commercial plant, as well as a mine, an oil well and the like. This is the reason why the above examples are listed in the permanent establishment definition that has been elaborated by the OECD within its MTC. A brick-and-mortar permanent establishment.

The permanent establishment is not a separate body from the non-resident taxpayer, whether an individual entrepreneur or, in most cases, a corporation. It is part of the non-resident corporation; better, it is its "longa manus" in the State of source.

G. Marino, *The Dark Side of International Tax Law*,
https://doi.org/10.1007/978-3-032-08159-9_9

This is the reason why the permanent establishment cannot be resident in the State of source; it can only be located in the State of source, since the only legal entity entitled to be qualified as resident or non-resident is the corporation.

The permanent establishment must not be confused with the main business activity of the corporation, which is used in some tax jurisdictions as one of the criteria to determine corporate tax residence. Intuitively, the permanent establishment is smaller than the main business activity, and it is indeed only worth the perimeter of the business income for territorial taxation, while the location of the main business activity would bring about worldwide business income taxation.

Nevertheless, the permanent establishment brings some tax duties in the States of source as if it were a regular taxpayer: 1) it must have a legal representative in the State of source; 2) it must keep a regular accounting; 3) it must deposit its own "balance sheet", together with the official balance sheet of the corporation where its activity is separately evidenced.

1.1. Article 5 of the Organisation for Economic Co-operation and Development (OECD) Model Tax Convention (MTC) provides for (i) a general definition of permanent establishment, (ii) a positive list of material permanent establishments, (iii) a negative list of material permanent establishments and (iv) a definition of personal permanent establishment.

The article states:

1. For the purposes of this Convention, the term "permanent establishment" means a fixed place of business through which the business of an enterprise is wholly or partly carried on.
2. The term "permanent establishment" includes especially:
   a) a place of management;
   b) a branch;
   c) an office;
   d) a factory;
   e) a workshop, and
   f) a mine, an oil or gas well, a quarry or any other place of extraction of natural resources.
3. A building site or construction or installation project constitutes a permanent establishment only if it lasts more than twelve months.
4. Notwithstanding the preceding provisions of this Article, the term "permanent establishment" shall be deemed not to include:
   a) the use of facilities solely for the purpose of storage, display or delivery of goods or merchandise belonging to the enterprise;
   b) the maintenance of a stock of goods or merchandise belonging to the enterprise solely for the purpose of storage, display or delivery;
   c) the maintenance of a stock of goods or merchandise belonging to the enterprise solely for the purpose of processing by another enterprise;
   d) the maintenance of a fixed place of business solely for the purpose of purchasing goods or merchandise or of collecting information, for the enterprise;
   e) the maintenance of a fixed place of business solely for the purpose of carrying on, for the enterprise, any other activity;
   f) the maintenance of a fixed place of business solely for any combination of activities mentioned in subparagraphs a) to e),

   provided that such activity or, in the case of subparagraph f), the overall activity of the fixed place of business, is of a preparatory or auxiliary character.

It is worth noting that the case of a building site, a construction or an installation project constitutes a permanent establishment only if its presence in the State of source is more than 12 months. This is a compromise recommended by the OECD since the State of residence has an interest in its business commitment staying in the State of source as long as possible without constituting a permanent establishment so that its worldwide taxation would be the sole taxation. The State of the source has the opposite interest; the shorter the time for the business commitment of the non-resident taxpayer to be qualified as a permanent establishment, the better it is, since it would bring, therefore, territorial taxation. The 2025 update of OECD MTC revises the Commentary to give detailed guidance and examples to assess whether an employee's home (or other "relevant place" like holiday flat, relative's home, second residence etc.) in a different country than the employer may constitute a "fixed place of business" for the employer. The determination must be based on facts and circumstances, i.e. permanence, frequency, the nature of activities, and business-related reasons.

1.2. It is understandable that the way to do business all over the globalised world is in constant evolution, and therefore, these rules could not work properly for the States of source to catch their portion of business income taxation. This is the reason why the OECD decided to amend the rules starting from 2015.

There are three main changes:

1. *Warehouse*: is a warehouse sufficient to have a permanent establishment in a country? No, it is included in the negative list, but there are cases in which it is necessary to make an exception. Example: Amazon. If a warehouse is the *core business* (is the most important link that Amazon has in the State of source), then it is sufficient to have a permanent establishment in that country.
2. *Anti-fragmentation rule*: companies belonging to a multinational group (which resides in country A) have different presences in Country B that, if considered singularly, do not qualify as permanent establishments (e.g. things that belong to the negative list of Permanent Establishment [PE]). However, an overlook of all the activities performed in Country B by all the companies together could result in a permanent establishment, regardless of whether the business activity is divided into many parts.
3. *Agent permanent establishment*: the OECD states that if you have a person in a foreign country trying to sell your products, then in that case you have an agent PE even if he doesn't work *on behalf of* the foreign company.

1.3. Finally, the invasion of the digital economy within the globalised world through digital giants like Apple, Amazon, Meta (Facebook), Google, Netflix, Spotify and Alibaba. The issue here is whether the traditional definition of permanent establishment adopted by the OECD MTC can capture the business activity that these digital companies perform in the State of sources, namely in their market destinations. Not at all.

For example: Netflix. It is a tax resident in the US but conducts business in Italy. Is Netflix able to do business in Italy? Yes, by selling products on online platforms.

Netflix does not have an office or a branch in Italy, so there is no permanent establishment. Nevertheless, they can do business in Italy, thanks to the platform. In this case, traditional rules do not make a connection between Italy and Netflix.

There is a need to add a new definition, the so-called digital permanent establishment, when a non-resident corporation has significant economic presence in the State of source, without having a material presence there, an office, or working people. How can digital presence be defined? One criterion could be the location of customers who have contracts with a digital company. The connection to the territory may be linked to the location of users through the IP address. However, this is only an idea.

The discussion is ongoing at the international level, and there is still a lot of confusion. The OECD is working on it, but it is hard to find a compromise between the State of residence of the digital giants (the US) and the States of market destination (the European Union, EU).

9.2 BEPS 2.0: The Geopolitics of Global Tax Reform

In an era defined by digital globalization and widening inequality, the international tax system has been stretched to its limits. As multinational enterprises (MNEs) increasingly earned profits in countries where they had no physical presence, governments around the world saw their tax bases erode. At the heart of the response to this problem lies Base Erosion and Profit Shifting (BEPS) 2.0 of the OECD/G20 Inclusive Framework and its two central reforms: Pillar 1 and Pillar 2.

These so-called "two pillars" represent the most ambitious effort in decades to reshape global tax rules. But beyond the technical frameworks and regulatory blueprints, they tell a deeper story—one of geopolitical struggle, compromise, and the enduring challenge of cooperation in a divided world.

2.1. The first pillar seeks to modernize the rules regarding where profits are taxed. Specifically, it proposes that countries where consumers and users are located, even if companies have no physical presence there, should be entitled to tax a share of large MNEs' profits.

The OECD's Pillar 1 proposal, first introduced in 2019 and agreed upon in principle in October 2021, was designed to defuse the conflict. It offered a multilateral approach: in return for withdrawing their national Digital Services Taxes (DSTs), countries would receive a new taxing right (called Amount A) over a slice of the residual profits of the largest MNEs.

However, the implementation has failed. The proposal requires a Multilateral Convention (MLC) to be signed and ratified by many countries, including the United States. Here, domestic politics have intervened. Despite initial support from the Biden administration, US lawmakers across the political spectrum have expressed scepticism. Without US ratification, the entire framework risks unravelling.

Meanwhile, developing countries have voiced dissatisfaction with the limited scope of Pillar 1. Many argue that the rules benefit rich consumer economies and still allow headquarters jurisdictions to retain the most taxing rights. As of 2025, despite years of negotiation, Pillar 1 remains stuck in the purgatory of diplomatic hesitation.

2.2. While Pillar 1 tackles who gets to tax, Pillar 2 focuses on how much tax MNEs should pay. It introduces a global minimum corporate tax rate of 15%, intended to combat profit shifting and end the "race to the bottom" among countries competing to offer the lowest tax rates.

This idea gained unexpected momentum. The European Union, long a champion of coordinated tax reform, rallied behind it. The Biden administration also voiced strong support, seeing it as part of a broader domestic agenda to increase corporate tax fairness. Even traditional low-tax jurisdictions, like Ireland, ultimately joined the agreement, though not without resistance.

However, Pillar 2 has faced geopolitical and technical hurdles of its own. The US is yet to align its domestic tax code with the OECD model, and many countries in the Global South have expressed concerns that the benefits of the global minimum tax will primarily accrue to wealthy nations. Under the current structure, top-up taxes are often paid to the parent company's home jurisdiction, meaning that profits earned in Africa or Asia may be taxed in Europe or North America.

Despite these issues, Pillar 2 has advanced further than its counterpart. The European Union formally adopted the rules in 2022, and countries such as the UK, Japan and South Korea began implementing them in 2024. A critical mass is forming, with large multinationals beginning to adjust their tax structures in anticipation.

9.3 The Road Ahead: Cooperation in a Fractured Landscape

Together, Pillars 1 and 2 reflect the most coordinated attempts over decades to rebuild global tax rules in the digital era. But they also expose deep fault lines in global economic governance: between developed and developing countries, between multilateralism and unilateral action, and between domestic political pressures and international compromise.

Pillar 2 is becoming a reality, albeit with imperfections. Pillar 1 remains an idea caught in the tangle between geopolitics and legislative inertia. Both efforts, however, highlight a critical truth: global problems require global solutions—and those solutions must be equitable, enforceable, and politically viable.

As the world watches to see if these reforms can withstand the weight of their ambitions, one thing is clear: the global tax debate is far from over. Countries, like France, Italy, India and the UK, have introduced unilateral digital services taxes, targeting US-based tech giants such as Google and Facebook. These measures were seen as necessary stopgaps in the absence of an international solution—but they sparked trade tensions with the United States, which accused allies of unfairly singling out American firms.

Some States of source are also introducing, on a unilateral basis, a definition of digital permanent establishment with an anti-abuse scope to preserve their revenue in case no traditional permanent establishment appears. This is the case in Italy, which has introduced a digital permanent establishment definition. Article 162, c. 2, lett. f-bis), of Italian Tax Code (ITC), states that it is a permanent establishment, a significant and continuous economic presence in the Italian territory, built in such a way as not to make it appear a material presence. This approach impedes tax treaty protection for the non-resident taxpayer; no treaty, indeed, could justify a tax avoidance scheme in the name of the elimination of double taxation.

References

Kane MA (2015) A defense of source rules in international taxation. Yale J Reg 32:311
Kobetsky M (2011) International taxation of permanent establishments. Cambridge Tax Law Series
Maisto G (ed) (2019) New trends in the definition of permanent establishment, EC and International Tax Law Series. IBFD
OECD (2020) Tax challenges arising from digitalization - economic impact assessment. Paris
Shay SE, Clifton Fleming Jr J, Peroni RJ (2002–2003) The David R. Tillinghast Lecture "What's Source Got to Do With It?" Source Rules and U.S. International Taxation. Tax Law Rev 56:81
Skaar AA (2020) Permanent establishment: erosion of a tax treaty principle. Wolters Kluwer
Turina A (2018) Which "source taxation" for the digital economy? Intertax 46(6/7)

Chapter 10
Outbound Taxation

Contents

10.1 Introduction

Within outbound taxation, the perspective is that of the State of residence, where international taxation begins, with reference to taxpayers sending money, making investments and performing their activities abroad.

There is no distinction between passive and active income for resident taxpayers; everything must be reported in the tax return, which generally implies the application of progressive tax rates for individuals and proportional tax rates for corporations.

Worldwide income taxation of the State of residence brings a juridical (or legal) double taxation, which is when the same taxpayer must pay tax on the same income both in the State of source and in the State of residence, with a clear breach of the ability-to-pay principle in the State of residence. According to the Report on Double Taxation of 1923, the State of residence must eliminate juridical (or legal) double taxation by way of foreign tax credit or by way of the exemption method.

Beyond juridical (or legal) double taxation, economic double taxation also arises in the State of residence when its resident taxpayers receive dividends from non-resident corporations out of profits that have already been taxed with the corporate income tax in their State of residence. It should be the duty of the State of residence of shareholders to eliminate the economic double taxation by way of an underlying

G. Marino, *The Dark Side of International Tax Law*,
https://doi.org/10.1007/978-3-032-08159-9_10

foreign tax credit or by way of exempting dividends from domestic income tax. Economic double taxation jeopardizes international business, which is the reason why the international community supports the elimination of both kinds of double taxation.

10.2 The Foreign Tax Credit (FTC)

The idea behind the foreign tax credit (FTC) goes back over a century. In the early 1900s, as American businesses started expanding overseas—building factories, selling products, and making money in other countries—a problem quickly emerged. The US wanted to tax its citizens on their worldwide income, but the countries where that income was earned did so. The result? Double taxation—and companies weren't happy.

To stay competitive and fair, governments needed a solution. So, in 1918, the United States became the first country to introduce a formal foreign tax credit. The goal was simple: if you paid income taxes abroad, you could subtract those taxes from what you were obliged to pay at home.

This idea quickly spread. Over time, other countries—especially those with global business interests—adopted similar measures, either unilaterally or through tax treaties with other nations.

2.1. As international trade and investment grew in the twentieth century, so did the need for cooperation on tax issues. FTC became part of a broader system of international tax coordination. Organizations like the League of Nations (the precursor to the United Nations [UN]) first discussed how to divide taxing rights in the 1920s. Later, the Organisation for Economic Co-operation and Development (OECD) Model Tax Convention—a blueprint for tax treaties used by over 100 countries—promoted two key methods to avoid double taxation: (i) the exemption method, in which a country simply does not tax certain foreign income, and (ii) the credit method, in which a country taxes foreign income but gives credit for taxes already paid abroad, and this is foreign tax credit.

By the late twentieth century, the FTC had become a cornerstone of international tax policy, helping multinational companies operate across borders without being punished by overlapping tax systems. FTC may sound technical, but it plays a major role in how modern global business works. It's about fairness—making sure people and companies do not get taxed twice on the same income. But it's also about balance—letting countries collect the taxes they're owed, without discouraging investment and trade. As the global economy evolves, so too will the Foreign Tax Credit. But its original purpose—to reduce barriers between nations—remains as relevant as ever.

2.2. Imagine a corporate taxpayer resident in Italy that produces an income of 10,000 euro in Greece. Greece applies a corporate income tax of €2,000, considering that the Italian corporate taxpayer has a permanent establishment in its territory. Back in Italy, the company must also pay corporate tax (IRES) on that income. But thanks to the FTC, the taxpayer may be able to subtract the €2,000 already paid in Greece from the Italian tax bill. There are, of course, rules and limits. It can never happen to claim a credit for more tax than that owed at home. And only certain kinds of taxes—usually income taxes—qualify. Still, it is a powerful way to level the playing field.

For example, in today's digital and global economies, companies may operate in dozens of countries simultaneously. Individuals can work remotely across borders. Digital giants can earn income in places where they have no office at all. Because of digitalization that leaves active businesses disappearing from the screen radar of the State of source, being the market jurisdiction, and the impending collapse of Pillar 1 of the OECD's base erosion and profit shifting 2.0 project, many countries, like Austria, France, Italy, Spain and the UK, introduced digital services taxes (DSTs). DSTs are popular for three reasons: (i) they are fair, since they are perceived as enabling market jurisdictions to tax US digital giants earning billions in profits in their territories while avoiding local income taxes because of limits imposed by tax treaties; (ii) they are efficient, since imposing a tax on the digital monopolistic giants does not significantly change its behaviour because in most cases it was already able to charge the maximum price the market would bear before the imposition of the tax; (iii) they are revenue source, since they raise significant revenue from non-voters and therefore the saying "don't tax you, don't tax me, tax the fellow behind the tree" (declaration attributed to Sen. Russell B. Long, who chaired the Senate Finance Committee of the US Congress from 1966 to 1981).

According to Reuven Avi-Yonah, DSTs should be creditable under Section 903 of the US Income Tax Code because (i) they are normally borne by the shareholders of corporate taxpayers, not by consumers or advertisers, and (ii) they are a valid in-lieu-of tax for the net income tax that should have been imposed on corporate taxpayers but for the Permanent Establishment (PE) limitation. The attribution rule, which seeks to deny credibility, does not have a statutory basis and should be withdrawn.

10.3 The Tax-Sparing Clauses

Some governments are tightening rules around FTCs to prevent abuse. In some cases, companies structure their operations in tax havens to claim large credits on small taxes or, better, to claim the benefit of tax-sparing clauses under tax treaties—something regulators are working hard to stop.

A tax-sparing clause is a provision within a bilateral tax treaty that allows a taxpayer to benefit from a foreign tax credit in its resident State for taxes that were waived or reduced in the State of source where the income was earned. In other words, the investor receives credit as if the foreign tax had been paid, even if, due to a tax incentive, no actual tax was levied in the country of source. This is best illustrated through the concept of "tax sparing"—the idea that the State of residence "spares" tax by allowing a credit for tax that the State of source has forgone as part of an incentive scheme.

Tax-sparing clauses emerged after World War II during a period of decolonization and reconstruction and became more widespread during the 1970s and the 1980s, as developing countries sought to stimulate growth by attracting foreign direct investment (FDI). The logic behind these clauses is based on the concern that if a developing country provides tax holidays or exemptions to attract investment, these incentives become pointless if the investor's home country taxes the income fully anyway. This is known as the neutralization problem—when the tax relief granted by a host country is "neutralized" by the home country's tax system.

Tax sparing solves this by allowing the investor's home country to pretend that the foreign tax was paid, granting credit against domestic tax liability, thereby preserving the effectiveness of the developing country's incentives.

The concept of tax sparing gained traction with the OECD Model Convention (1963) and later found support in the UN Model Tax Convention, which was more favourable to developing countries. While the OECD Model does not recommend tax sparing, especially in more recent versions, reflecting developed countries' reluctance, the UN Model supports tax sparing as a legitimate development policy tool.

3.1. Tax-sparing provisions became a common feature of North-South treaties (e.g. UK–India, Japan–Philippines, France–Senegal), often reflecting political and developmental motives as much as purely fiscal considerations. Italy is a capital-exporting country, and its tax system generally follows the credit method for avoiding double taxation. Under this system, Italy allows credit for foreign taxes paid on foreign income up to the amount of Italian tax due on that income. However, if the foreign country grants a tax holiday or exemption, no tax is paid, and no credit can be granted unless a tax-sparing clause applies. Italy has traditionally been cautious with tax sparing, aligning more closely with OECD recommendations, which discourage broad use due to abuse risks. However, in the context of development cooperation and strategic partnerships, Italy has agreed to include tax sparing in select treaties.

Here are some notable examples where tax sparing or tax credit preservation mechanisms have been included in Italy's bilateral treaties: (A) India–Italy Tax Treaty (1993). The India–Italy Treaty contains a classic tax-sparing clause under Article 23 (Elimination of Double Taxation). Italy grants a tax credit not only for tax actually paid in India but also for Indian tax that has been reduced or exempted under Indian laws for the purpose of promoting economic development. This provision is crucial for encouraging Italian investment in the Indian infrastructure, manufacturing, and tech sectors. (B) Philippines–Italy Treaty (1980) Another traditional case: the treaty allows Italy to grant a tax credit for taxes "spared" under Philippine development incentives. The treaty text specifies that Italy shall credit tax which "would have been payable under Philippine law but was reduced or waived under incentives to promote development". This treaty is part of Italy's broader engagement with Southeast Asia and fits within its developmental aid priorities in the

1980s. (C) China–Italy Treaty (1986, amended 2019). In the older version of the China–Italy tax treaty, Italy recognized tax incentives granted under Chinese domestic law. While the 2019 protocol modernized many aspects, it phased out automatic tax sparing, reflecting the changing Chinese tax environment and Italy's cautious stance. That said, some grandfathering provisions may still apply to certain investments. (D) Vietnam–Italy Treaty (1996). This treaty also includes tax-sparing provisions, especially relevant in the 1990s, when Vietnam was liberalizing its economy. Italy recognized Vietnam's right to use tax holidays to attract investment and granted credit accordingly.

3.2. Tax-sparing clauses—once hailed as tools of developmental solidarity—are today subject to growing criticism, both from a tax policy and a practical enforcement standpoint. Over the past two decades, these provisions have been increasingly scrutinized, especially in the wake of global efforts to combat base erosion, profit shifting (BEPS) and treaty abuse. The biggest concern with tax-sparing clauses is that they are vulnerable to abuse through treaty shopping—a practice where investors route their income through jurisdictions with the most favourable tax treaties, even if they have no substantial activity there. (i) An investor from Country A wants to invest in Country C, but Country A does not have a favourable treaty; (ii) the investor sets up a holding company in Country B, which has a tax treaty with Country C that includes a tax-sparing clause; (iii) Country C grants a tax holiday, and Country B grants a tax credit as if tax were paid—even though it wasn't and (iv) the investor benefits from zero or minimal tax, despite having no economic substance in Country B. This erodes tax bases and undermines the developmental purpose for which tax incentives were originally offered.

The India–Mauritius Treaty (before its 2016 amendment) allowed for such exploitation, thus becoming a textbook case of treaty misuse, as the Vodafone case demonstrates. Capital gain exemptions and tax sparing were widely used by global investors—not just Mauritian companies—to route funds into tax-free India.

Tax sparing requires assumptions about what tax "would have been paid" in the absence of an incentive. This raises several problems: (i) difficult to audit, since Tax Authorities in the State of residence must verify what would have been paid under hypothetical scenarios; (ii) changing tax laws, since if the State of source frequently alters its tax incentives, it becomes difficult to determine the "baseline" tax liability; (iii) information asymmetry, when the Tax Administration of the State of residence lacks access to the State of source incentive laws, making compliance subjective.

In practice, this opens the door to errors, inconsistencies, and potential manipulation. BEPS 1.0 calls for greater transparency, substance, and anti-abuse mechanisms in international taxation. Tax-sparing clauses are seen by many as incompatible with this philosophy.

10.4 Controlled Foreign Companies (CFC) Legislation

However, when economic double taxation still exists, resident taxpayers, particularly corporations, may find it convenient not to receive dividends from their foreign subsidiaries so as to induce an income tax deferral until the dividends are distributed, which could mean never paying taxes in their State of residence. If the corporation that should distribute dividends does not pay income tax in its State of residence, from economic double taxation, another scenario arises: the economic double non-taxation.

In the United States, the Kennedy Administration decided to fight the case of tax deferral and double non-taxation by introducing controlled foreign companies' legislation (CFC) in 1962 with the scope to pierce the foreign corporate veil and tax its income as if it were the income of the US controlling company, without waiting for dividend distribution. It is like saying that the company becomes tax transparent since its profit is automatically income of the shareholder. The US experience has been imported into other countries: Germany (1972), Canada (1975), Japan (1978), France (1980), the UK (1984), Italy (2001) and 20 other countries.

4.1. The conditions to apply CFC legislation depend on how a single jurisdiction has decided to implement it; however, the following aspect can be described in general terms.

The first is the control of foreign companies. Formal control occurs when there is a 50% + 1 share in the company. This means that shareholders can decide whether to distribute dividends or not. The US approach is one of formal control. Alternatively, substantial control occurs when the shareholder has less than 50% + 1 shares, but there is a substantial influence on society (i.e. the two main shareholders are brothers or spouses). Substantial control requires greater effort for the revenue to catch it (it is easier to assess formal control).

4.2. The second is the US global/transactional approach. Once there is control, US CFC legislation states that tax transparency applies to all controlled companies outside the US, regardless of whether they reside in an offshore country or in a country with a high tax burden. Once there is control over a foreign corporation, it becomes a CFC. The consequence of the transactional approach is that the income of the controlled company that must be taxed at the level of the controlling company is only passive income (portfolio income, including dividends, interest and royalties), while there is no need to pierce the corporate veil transactionally for active income, namely, business and commercial activity. This is the reason why if you have a foreign corporation having both, the US CFC legislation only applies to passive income, and active income is going to be taxed only when the related dividends are distributed. This brings us back to understanding what is active and what is passive, having in mind that the Revenue of the State of residence is to find passive income that is sheltered as active income.

Everything started in 1994 in the US. Why? US multinational enterprises (MNEs) used to have corporations outside the US. These MNEs started lobbying the US

Administration to avoid the concept of passive income and to confuse the idea of passive income with active income: the more active the income, the better it is because tax-free money can be held out of the country insofar as dividends need to be repatriated. In December 1996, lobbies obtained from the US Treasury an interpretation of the CFC legislation to make exemptions to passive income and to transform passive into active (the so-called "check-the-box" rule as part of Treasury Regulation & 301.7701-1 through & 301.7701-3). The result was that from 1994 to 2017, the US discovered that abroad, there were 3 trillion US dollars not taxed into companies outside the country controlled by MNEs, whose income was called active, but it was passive. They used new technologies to transform passive into active. They used royalties and created copyrights (which are passive). The shares of US MNEs quoted at the stock exchange were reflecting the cash kept abroad, so the value of the shares was growing because no tax was paid (Wall Street does not need dividends because investors may sell the shares through buy-backs when their value rise by realizing long term capital gains).

The problem arose in 2013 in Europe when Margrethe Vestager, the European Union (EU) Commissioner for antitrust, wanted to tax those 3 trillion because they were generated in the European market by the tech giants. This is the beginning of the Apple case (ECJ 10 September 2024, C-465/20 P) that ended with the victory of the EU Commission: Apple had to give 12 billion US dollars back in Irish tax benefits to Europe. Once the US understood that Europe started to hide the money offshore, Trump reacted in 2017, saying, "That money is our money", but Margrethe Vestager disagreed. Trump made an offer to US MNEs to bring the money in iCloud back to the US. Under his Administration, the US Congress promoted a repatriation tax at the rate of 15.5% instead of the ordinary 30% tax rate in the case of dividend distributions, while if there are no cash but intangible assets, they could be repatriated at the rate of 8%.

This is the beauty of tax competition. There are other tax rules established by the Trump Administration in order to keep the money of the digital economy in the US under the slogan 'America first', and it seems that MNEs found it convenient to repatriate the money, pay a lower percentage of tax and bring the money abroad again.

4.3. Under the jurisdictional approach (applied, e.g. in Japan and Italy), once there is control, it is important to look at the place where the company is located. If the controlled company is not in an offshore country with low tax jurisdiction, the company shall not be a CFC, and if it is not a CFC, the ordinary system of tax deferral applies, regardless of any distinction between passive and active income. To check whether the company is in an offshore country, countries provide a blacklist of offshore countries or, alternatively, a whitelist. Depending on the evolution of each single tax jurisdiction, a country can move from blacklists to whitelists and the other way round. At today, the most salient sets of blacklists relevant to tax and financial transparency are (i) the EU list of non-cooperative tax jurisdictions; (ii) national blacklists by individual countries such Tax Authorities; (iii) blacklists of bodies like the Financial Action Task Force (FATF) focusing on financial-secrecy/anti-money laundering and terrorism financing risk rather than strictly "tax" issues.

References

OECD (2015) Designing effective controlled foreign company rules. Paris

Oner C (2024) An analysis of controlled foreign company rules, the OECD's pillar two and developing countries. Bull Int Tax 1

Schouen PGL, Galendi Jùnior RA (2024) CFCs and tax treaties: historical elements for the IIR debate. Intertax 52(1)

Chapter 11
The Transfer Pricing

Contents

11.1 Preamble

The jurisdiction to tax focuses on who has the right to tax; inbound and outbound taxation focus on what to tax (passive or active income) and how to tax (withholding or tax return); and the transfer pricing legislation has the scope to determine how much to tax. This legislation, as well as Controlled Foreign Corporation (CFC), is addressed to those MNEs operating in more than one country through so-called "related companies", being subsidiaries. The importance of transfer pricing has to do with the assumption that corporate income taxes (CITs) differ from country to country, and there might be a temptation for MNEs to make transactions with each other that do not reflect the real value of the goods and services being transferred.

In today's interconnected global economy, where multinational enterprises (MNEs) span dozens of jurisdictions and shift billions in profits, transfer pricing sits at the heart of the global tax debate. But this complex system—used to determine the prices at which related companies transact across borders—has humble origins rooted in corporate accounting. Its transformation into a central pillar of international tax law reflects decades of legal innovation, economic theory, and geopolitical tension.

G. Marino, *The Dark Side of International Tax Law*,
https://doi.org/10.1007/978-3-032-08159-9_11

11.2 Early Origins: Managing Internal Transactions

The concept of transfer pricing dates back to the early twentieth century, when large corporations began operating with internal divisions spread across different regions. These firms needed a method to allocate profits between branches for performance assessment and internal decision-making.

Initially, transfer prices were simply tools of management accounting. Companies used them to incentivize performance, track internal costs, and evaluate divisional efficiency. Taxation wasn't a primary concern—at least not yet.

As global trade expanded in the post–World War II era, multinational companies became increasingly sophisticated. By the 1960s and the 1970s, Tax Authorities began noticing that MNEs were using intercompany transactions—particularly involving intangibles, services, and royalties—to shift profits to low-tax jurisdictions. The potential for base erosion and profit shifting (BEPS) became clear.

In response, governments began crafting rules to ensure that related-party transactions are priced as if they were between unrelated parties. This principle became known as the "arm's length principle"—the foundation of modern transfer pricing.

11.3 The OECD Steps in Establishing the Global Standard

In 1979, the Organisation for Economic Co-operation and Development (OECD) issued its first Transfer Pricing Guidelines, formalizing the arm's length principle and providing guidance to governments on how to evaluate whether transfer prices between related entities reflect market conditions.

These guidelines have been expanded and updated over the years, notably as follows:

- 1995: A major revision of the OECD Transfer Pricing Guidelines clarified accepted methods (e.g. Comparable Uncontrolled Price, Resale Price and Cost Plus) and laid out documentation requirements.
- 2000s: New guidance on intangibles, cost-sharing arrangements, and financial transactions emerged as tax planning became more complex.

At the same time, US Treasury regulations under Internal Revenue Code (IRC) Section 482, first issued in the 1960s and updated in the 1990s, also became highly influential. These rules provide detailed guidance on pricing methods, comparability, and adjustments.

By the early 2000s, it was evident that many MNEs—especially in the tech and pharmaceutical sectors—were using transfer pricing to minimize global tax liabilities. Structures involving intellectual property (IP) licensing, royalty payments and contract manufacturing allowed companies to legally shift profits to jurisdictions with little or no tax.

Some famous cases include (i) Google's "Double Irish": used to route billions in royalties through Ireland and the Caribbean; (ii) Apple's IP arrangements: shifted profits away from the US through Irish subsidiaries and (iii) Starbucks and Amazon in the European Union (EU): investigated favourable tax rulings that relied on questionable transfer pricing models.

These practices have triggered public outrage and investigations by Tax Authorities and policymakers across the globe.

11.4 BEPS 1.0 and the Reinvention of Transfer Pricing

In 2013, amid growing concerns about tax base erosion, the OECD and G20 launched the Base Erosion and Profit Shifting (BEPS) Project—a sweeping initiative to close loopholes in international tax rules.

BEPS 1.0 introduced significant changes to transfer pricing, including

- BEPS Action 8–10: Tightened rules on intangibles, risk allocation, and contractual arrangements.
- BEPS Action 13: Mandated country-by-country reporting (CbCR) and expanded documentation requirements to enhance transparency.

The result was a shift towards substance over form. Tax Authorities were now expected to scrutinize whether a company's transfer pricing truly reflected the location of its economic activity, people, and assets, not just contractual labels.

Debates over transfer pricing did not end with BEPS. As digital businesses continued to earn substantial profits with limited physical presence, the arm's length principle itself came under fire. This led to the introduction of the OECD's Pillar 1 and Pillar 2 initiatives: (i) Pillar 1 partially abandons the arm's length principle for certain large companies, reallocating profits based on market presence, and (ii) Pillar 2, which imposes a 15% global minimum tax, reduces the incentive to shift profits using aggressive transfer pricing.

Meanwhile, enforcement has intensified more audits as well as increased litigation (e.g. Coca-Cola Co. v. Commissioner, 2 August 2024, n. 31183-15, for a $3 billion tax dispute) and the growth of Advanced Pricing Agreements (APAs) and mutual agreement procedures (MAPs) to avoid double taxation.

11.5 Conclusion: Transfer Pricing at Crossroads

What began as a managerial tool for internal accounting has evolved into one of the most critical—and contested—mechanisms in global tax law. Transfer pricing remains rooted in the arm's length principle, but the world around it is changing. Calls for formulary apportionment, destination-based taxes, and more aggressive global coordination signal that the traditional model may not hold forever.

Still, transfer pricing endures. It balances national tax sovereignty with multinational business realities. It reflects the tension between form and substance, legality and fairness and principle and politics. As the global economy continues to evolve, so too will the way nations draw the lines around taxable profit.

11.6 In the Details of Transfer Pricing

For example, corporate income tax in the US has a tax rate of 21%, while in Europe, the lowest tax rate is in Ireland at 12.5%, while in Italy, it is 24%.

Assume that corporate income tax (tax applied on the income produced by corporations) in country A is 30%, while corporate income tax in country B is 20%. Hence, CIT in country B is lower than in country A.

Case of *related companies* (A and B are related even if the corporations are in different countries): the corporation in country A owns 100% of the corporation in country B, so corporation A controls corporation B (there are also other ways to control a company: influence because of contractual conditions, even if there is no shareholding).

Business: Shoes (Fig. 11.1).

Corporations in Country A must buy raw materials (milk) and transform them into final products (mozzarella cheese). Then, it sells the final product to the controlled company in country B, which is the sales corporation. Raw material is bought at a price of 20, and the final client buys the mozzarella cheese for 100 (this is the market price).

The parent company (male corporation) may decide to sell the mozzarella cheese to the sales company at the same price as the raw materials (20), which means a cost of 20 and a gross receipt of 20. Then, the sales corporation sells the mozzarella

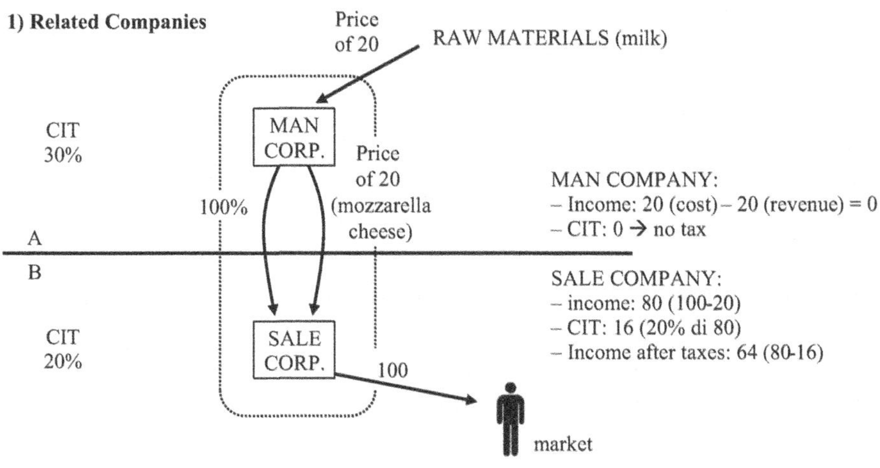

Fig. 11.1 Cross-border transactions without transfer pricing rules

cheese to the market at 100. Hence, the manufacturing company has zero income (because its revenue is 20 and its cost is 20, and 20-20 is 0, so it has 0 CIT), while the sales corporation has 80 income (100-20), the CIT is 16 and so the net income after taxes is 64 (80-16). Imagine the same transaction between *unrelated companies*. The company manufacturing the mozzarella cheese buys raw materials for 20 and sells to the unrelated sale corporation its product for 40, while the sale corporation in turn sells at 100 (the mozzarella cheese is the same). The result is that the male corporation has 20 of income, 6 CIT and 20 – 6 = 14 net income. The sales corporation has 60 of income, 12 CIT and 60 – 12 = 48 net income (Fig. 11.2).

How come that the same mozzarella cheese and raw materials (milk) generate different situations? In one case, the CIT is paid only in country B, and in the other case, the CIT is paid in both country A and country B. In the first case, there are related companies, and in the second case, there are non-related companies. The temptation of MNEs is to shift the taxable base from a country with high taxation to a country with lower taxation (country B has a lower CIT than country A).

Transfer pricing has to do with the determination of the right market price at which goods and services are sold at the international level, even when there is an MNE acting in the market. This means that, first, the group must be determined, and then the market must be determined (competitors producing the same quality of mozzarella cheese) to make an analysis of comparable prices. Once the comparable has been identified, it will be possible to verify whether the group is underestimating the income in country A. So, according to the example, CIT should be + 6.

There are two major categories of transfer pricing methods to determine the arm's length value. The first category has to do with traditional and classical methods.

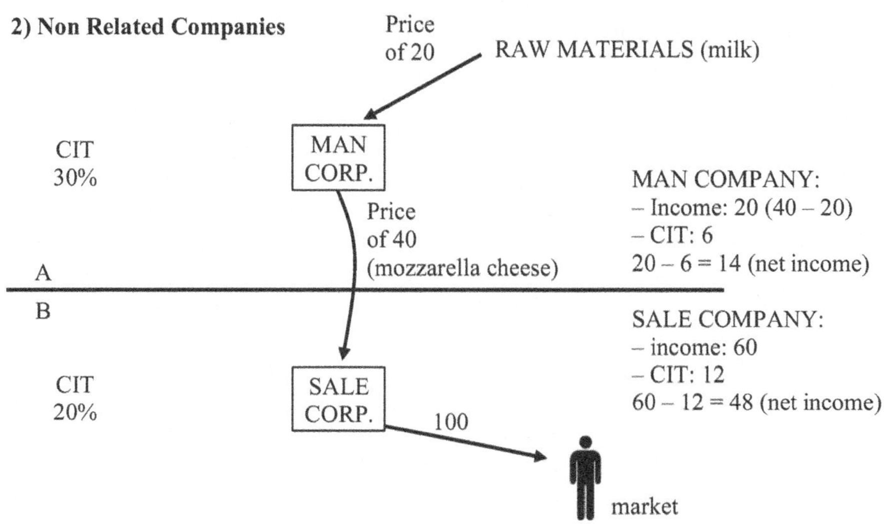

Fig. 11.2 Cross-border transactions with transfer-pricing rules

(i) *The Comparable Uncontrolled Price (CUP)* is the easiest method. In the example, the CUP is 40 by analysing the market and competitors selling the same products to determine the average price that will be the CUP. All competitors should be unrelated, and if they use different prices, an average must be calculated and compared with that of the group of companies.
(ii) *Cost Plus Method.* If it is difficult to determine the CUP, the arm's length price is determined by looking at the profitable margins of the producer exporting goods and services who wants to have them. 'Cost plus' refers to the profit margins of a category of competitors that shall be compared with the profit margin of the producer belonging to the group.
(iii) *Resale Price Method.* This is the opposite of the cost-plus method, since it looks at the profit margin of the company importing the goods and services for reselling them in its territory. The analysis uses the business sector of all distributors to discover their profit margin on average, to be compared with that of the distributor belonging to the group.

There is no priority in the use of the classical method; much depends on the situation.

Nowadays, it is still difficult to download mozzarella cheese, but because of the digitalization of the economy, many tangible assets are transformed into intangible assets, and many intangible assets are generating digital services. With the consequence that everything physically disappears, and it is difficult to ascertain the value of the services rendered and the connected price. For example, as far as the pharmaceutical sector is concerned, it is hard to understand how much the **Co**rona**vi**rus **D**isease 20**19** (COVID-19) vaccine costs and what its arm's length price should be because the political influence of governments is so strong that it creates a false idea of the market price.

This is the reason why, from classical methods, it is more frequent to shift to the second category, including more advanced methods based on profit analysis:

(i) *Comparable Profit Method* (CPM) or *Transactional Net Margin Method* (TNMM). Under the CPM/TNMM, the comparables are taken from industries other than that of the MNE under assessment but are considered similar industries. The theory at the base of these methods is that these margins will typically show a bell-shaped curve at which the 25% bottom and 25% top are eliminated, and the profit of the tested party is checked. If it falls within the remaining middle 50% of profits, the assessed MNE is immune from further challenges. However, economists working on CPM/TNMM find comparables of widely different industries, with the consequence that the number of claimed comparables found is too small to support a statistically useful bell curve.
(ii) *Profit Split Method* (PSM) does not require as many comparables since the functions of the related parties are assessed and a standard market-based return is assigned to each based on publicly available data. Any residual, which represents the extra profit earned by the MNE, is assigned to the developer or developers of the group's intangibles, since it is presumed that IP is responsible for the residual.

The future of the transfer pricing discipline is always a question mark. In theory, applying unitary taxation and formulary apportionment would likely yield a much more administrable and enforceable system, but for now, the OECD and many MNEs remain opposed to this practice. The idea to prevent tax litigations with advance pricing agreements (APAs) has not been successful either, since MNEs have won most decided transfer pricing cases since 1980, and even when APAs are concluded, they remain secret, giving rise to the perception that MNEs can enter hidden deals with Tax Authorities. Only a strong cross-border automatic exchange of information in country-by-country reports (CBCR) can create the necessary transparency in the determination of price mechanisms to induce MNEs to be more cooperative. But it is yet to come. The 2025 OECD MTC update explicitly deals with transfer pricing by revising the Commentaries (especially to Article 9) and aligning them with more recent global tax reforms (like Amount B and financing-transaction rules), the OECD intends to give better, more up-to-date guidance on how related-party transactions should be taxed across borders.

References

Baistrocchi E, Roxan I (eds) (2012) Resolving transfer pricing disputes: a global analysis. Cambridge University Press

Buriak S (2024) International taxation of global value networks. IBFD Doctoral Series

Collier RS, Andrus JL (2017) Transfer pricing and the arm's length principle after BEPS. Oxford University Press

Torvik O (2019) Transfer pricing and intangibles, IBFD Doctoral Series. IBFD

Treidler O (2020) Transfer pricing in one lesson. Springer

Verlinden I (2021) The value of a principle… the arm's length principle. Intertax 49(3)

Chapter 12
International Taxation as International Law

Contents

12.1 Preamble

International taxation occurs when a sovereign State asks for money to finance public expenses from its own taxpayers on their worldwide ability to pay, as well as from foreign taxpayers on their ability to pay that is located inside its territory. Once the Philosophy, Politics and Economics (PPE) of International Taxation is set and the ability to pay is ready to be captured (alternatively as wealth, income and/or consumption), the needs of international tax law appear.

Unfortunately, the international tax rules of a State might overlap with the set of rules adopted by other States where either the above abilities to pay or the taxpayers are located. This is the reason why international tax law is a two-faced Janus: on the one hand, domestic tax law is involved in the war, while on the other hand, international law, both treaty-based and customary, comes on stage for peace. Maybe it could be better to refer to Dr Jekyll and Mr Hyde since the international community generally plays for good, while single States play for evil.

Other sources of tax law may appear elsewhere, other than domestic and international sources. That is the case with the European sources of tax law because of the supranational organization being the European Union, which is between umbrellaing the 27 Member States before the rest of the world and influencing their international tax relations, both on a bilateral level as well as on a multilateral level.

G. Marino, *The Dark Side of International Tax Law*,
https://doi.org/10.1007/978-3-032-08159-9_12

There might be other similar sources of law, never experiencing the European Union (EU) superpower, like the Andean Pact in Latin America, North American Free Trade Agreement (NAFTA) in North America (e.g. Canada, the US and Mexico) and the Asian Pacific Trade Agreement (APTA) in the Far East.

1.1. In the other way around, sources of international taxation, such as international law, may be analysed by considering the idea of a condominium where each single legal owner of an apartment can do whatever he wants within his property (domestic area), but nevertheless needs to respect the rules of the condominium (international area). If the international community is a world condominium, then each single State may exercise tax sovereignty within its own territory but nevertheless needs to follow the rules of the world condominium every time its power to tax goes beyond its territory.

The primary rule to belong to the world condominium, namely the international community, is to be recognized as a State, and there are three elements to identify a State as a public sovereign entity: 1) population, 2) territory and 3) organization.

Certainly, States live in a world in which every single element is floating so rapidly that their identity is jeopardized. For example, the population today is fluctuating around the world through migration, and it is not easy to identify a population clearly (through language, religion, race, etc.). This is the reason why economic allegiance is easier than political allegiance. The same territory is no longer a clear concept; thus far, borders may vary depending on the perspective; there is a territory for Coronavirus Disease 2019 (COVID-19) purposes, another for the economy (especially the digital economy), and another for the law. Finally, the organization has rules and powers. The above three elements must be recognized by all other States belonging to the international community.

In his famous "Land and Sea" ("Land und Meer: Eine Weltgeschichtliche Betrachtung", 1942), Carl Schmitt argues that human history is tied to spatial structures, the way people organize, control and conceptualize space. He sees epochs of history marked by dominant spatial paradigms: 1) land-based empires (i.e. mediaeval Europe with feudal domains); 2) maritime empires (i.e. the rise of the British Empire, with global trade routes). The transition from one epoch to another involves a "Nomos" of the Earth, Schmitt's term for a world order grounded in a spatial-political arrangement. Though the book is centred on the land-sea dichotomy, Schmitt speculates that a new era is emerging since technology is transforming the nature of space and power, and the advent of air power may represent a new, third domain. Modern war and politics are moving toward total mobilization and a new kind of global spatial order. Today, this is the new world condominium.

As a consequence of the condominium concept, the sources of international taxation as international law may be divided into 1) domestic legal sources dealing with international taxation (based on national constitutions), 2) international legal sources dealing with international taxation (based on customary international law as accepted by national constitutions) and 3) European legal sources dealing with international taxation (based on the EU constitution as accepted by EU Member States' constitutions).

As far as international legal sources are concerned, each single State belonging to the international community follows customary international rules that seem to assume the role of an international constitution.

12.2 Beauty and Power of Customary Rules

Customary international law is the result of a general and consistent practice ("repetictio facti") of States followed by them from a sense of legal obligation ("opinio iuris sive necessitatis"). A sort of legally binding tradition. States believe, even if they don't know why, that there is a legal obligation to behave in a traditional way.

It is not easy to identify taxing behaviours that may be translated into customary international rules with a binding effect within the entire international community. Any following example of common traditional taxing practice, indeed, has dark sides that may jeopardize its customary nature:

- Jurisdiction to tax: It is a common practice at the international level that countries exercise their power to tax on resident taxpayers and non-resident taxpayers with a nexus within the country; however, the United States taxes its citizens regardless of where they are resident.
- Non-discrimination: A country cannot discriminate against two taxpayers because of the difference in residence. At the international level, there cannot be discrimination based on residence; however, in the field of tax competition, many States offer special tax regimes based on the acquisition of a tax residence, thus leading to discrimination.
- Arm's length principle: It is the philosophical cornerstone of transfer pricing legislation that many States of the international community use to determine how much tax a resident corporation must pay on its group cross-border transactions; however, there is no common standard understanding on the determination of the arm's length value methodology to which transfer pricing legislation must apply.
- Elimination of double taxation: The duty to eliminate domestic double taxation is in the will of any national constitution, while the need to avoid international double taxation is a simple wish since the 1923 Report on Double Taxation of the League of Nations and its methods to avoid the overlapping of taxing powers (tax credit and exemption method) are the core of tax treaties, and it is hard to determine that this wish is a common practice within the international community.
- Diplomatic tax immunity: The Latin "sanctum per saecula nomen legatus" means that ambassadors or consuls cannot be subject to income tax in the foreign State where they exercise their representative functions, and the same happens with embassies, consulates and properties, which cannot be subject to real property tax if they are owned by a foreign State. However, there is no common standard understanding at the international level of the attribution of the ambassador or consul status to individuals and real properties that could bring such a tax exemption, generating international tax conflicts.

2.1. During the Second World War, there were tensions in customary international law that were solved thanks to the Radbruch formula. Gustav Radbruch was a German philosopher studying human rights as natural rights, and his formula has been used in the context of the Nuremberg process, which was set up in an international auditorium to see whether the Nazis were guilty or not for what they did during the war.

Nazis said that they were obliged to kill people because of the domestic laws of their country. The American prosecutors were embarrassed because they realized that the Nazis were right, and they solved the issue by requesting the application of the Radbruch formula: customary international law provides not to violate human rights as natural rights, and that should also be above domestic law, so the Nazis should have contrasted domestic legislation obliging them to prosecute the Jewish people. The Radbruch formula belongs to customary international law, with the paradox that Nazis were condemned to the death penalty.

Finally, the most important example of customary international law is in another Latin broach, "pacta sunt servanda". The meaning is that if two countries belonging to the world condominium sign an agreement, namely a treaty, they are obliged to respect the contents of the treaty.

On 3 May 1969, the world condominium signed the Vienna Convention on the Law of Treaties. The Vienna Convention is the treaty of treaties, including tax treaties for the elimination of double taxation: it establishes the rules on how each single contracting State must behave when an international treaty is signed.

2.2. The contents of tax treaties always prevail over domestic tax legislation because treaties have a legal nature that is hierarchically superior to domestic tax laws for two reasons: 1) "ratione materiae", since the contents of a tax treaty are always more specific than any domestic tax law, dealing with the peculiarities of the two contracting States; and 2) the special procedure to reach the entry into force of a tax treaty, being very different from any other domestic tax law. First, the tax treaty needs to be negotiated by the government representatives of the two contracting States; second, the tax treaty must be signed by the government representatives and sent to the Parliaments; third, the Parliaments must approve a domestic law that authorizes the government to ratify the tax treaty with the representatives of the other contracting State; fourth, the legal instruments of ratification must be exchanged among the representatives; and fifth, the tax treaty enters into force after the ratification.

If a contracting State, after a tax treaty enters into force, unilaterally enacts domestic tax legislation that contradicts the contents of the tax treaty, there shall be a breach of "pacta sunt servanda" as customary international law, and that domestic tax law should not have binding effects, but only a judge may decide so.

Tax treaty overrides are unfortunately very frequent nowadays, not only from the side of the United States with the justification of arising national financial interests, but also from many other States of the international community with the justification that a tax treaty for the elimination of double taxation may be overriden in case the State enacts domestic legislation to protect its revenue from aggressive tax planning and, more generally, from double non-taxation.

12.3 The Conundrum of the European Union

The constitutional architecture of the European Union is a complex and unique system that blends elements of supranational governance with intergovernmental cooperation. At its core are foundational treaties, such as the Treaty of Rome and the Treaty on the European Union (Maastricht Treaty), which serve as the EU's de facto constitution. These treaties establish the division of competences between the EU and its Member States, outlining areas where the EU has exclusive authority, shared authority, or supportive roles.

The EU's institutions are designed to balance the interests of member states with the need for effective centralized governance. 1) The European Commission acts as the executive branch of the EU, responsible for proposing legislation, implementing decisions, enforcing EU law, and managing the day-to-day operations of the Union. It represents the interests of the EU as a whole. 2) The European Parliament is the directly elected legislative body, representing EU citizens. It shares legislative power with the Council of the European Union, approves the EU budget, and exercises democratic oversight of other EU institutions. 3) The Council of the European Union (often referred to as the Council) represents the governments of the Member States. It negotiates and adopts EU legislation in conjunction with the European Parliament and coordinates policies among Member States. 4) The European Council comprises the heads of state or government of the Member States and sets the EU's overall political direction and priorities. It does not have legislative functions but provides strategic guidance. 5) The Court of Justice of the European Union (CJEU) ensures the uniform interpretation and application of EU law across all Member States. It resolves legal disputes between member states, EU institutions, businesses, and individuals regarding the interpretation of EU law.

3.1. A complementary glue to the EU is the European Convention on Human Rights (ECHR), which is a foundational international treaty created in 1950 by the Council of Europe to protect basic human rights and freedoms in Europe. It was drafted in the aftermath of World War II with the aim of ensuring that such atrocities would never be repeated. The Convention sets out a list of civil and political rights—such as the right to life, prohibition of torture, right to a fair trial, freedom of expression and protection of property—which all member states are legally bound to respect.

To enforce these rights, the European Court of Human Rights (ECtHR) was established in 1959, based in Strasbourg, France. Individuals, groups, and even states can bring cases to the Court if they believe that a Member State has violated their rights under the Convention, but only after all domestic legal avenues have been exhausted. The Court's judgements are legally binding, and States must comply by changing laws or paying compensation when violations are found.

The ECHR and its Court form a cornerstone of the rule of law in Europe, influencing national laws and judicial decisions across the continent. They serve not only to protect individuals but also to harmonize human rights standards among the Council of Europe's 46 member states. Taxpayers' rights are clearly under the close monitoring of the ECtHR.

3.2. The principle of subsidiarity ensures that decisions are made as closely as possible to citizens, with the EU acting only when objectives cannot be sufficiently achieved by individual Member States. Additionally, the Charter of Fundamental Rights of the European Union provides a constitutional framework for protecting human rights within the Union. Together, these elements create a multi-layered system of governance that is constantly evolving to meet the challenges of integration and cooperation among its Member States.

The Treaty of Rome was fundamental in creating a common market within the European Union. This common market is a tariff-free zone that facilitates the free movement of goods, people, services, and capital. Over time, the European Union has evolved, and today, we also have a single currency, the euro.

To understand how tax regulations fit within the context of the European Union, it is important to know that international tax laws take precedence over national laws. These international laws are based on globally recognized customs and apply to tax treaties between countries.

3.3. The European Union consists of 27 Member States, each with its own national tax laws. But how do these laws relate to European tax law? We need to consider some fundamental principles of the Treaty on the Functioning of the European Union (TFEU) that also apply in the tax domain.

1. Article 26 TFEU—Freedom of Movement: This principle not only concerns the freedom of citizens to move and settle in another EU country but also applies to businesses and workers. People can freely relocate, work, and open bank accounts in any EU country without needing specific justifications.
2. Article 18 TFEU—Non-Discrimination: If a person can settle in another EU country, it is because there is no discrimination based on nationality. This principle ensures that there are no disadvantages for those who move from one Member State to another.
3. Article 28 TFEU—Customs Union: To create a common market, it is essential to eliminate customs duties and other trade barriers between Member States.
4. Article 107 TFEU—Prohibition of State Aid: This article prohibits Member States from granting aid to individual businesses if it distorts competition. State aid can create unfair advantages and compromise the common markets. Notable examples of state aid in Italy include Alitalia and Ilva.
5. Article 113 TFEU—Harmonization of Indirect Taxes: Indirect taxes, such as customs duties and tariffs, must be harmonized among member states to avoid distortions in the single market.

Regarding direct taxes, there is no fundamental principle that mandates their harmonization at the European level. Direct taxes are subject to a process of bringing jurisdictions closer together, but this decision requires unanimous votes to create a true fiscal union. If Member States disagree, harmonization cannot proceed.

There are cases in which the European Court of Justice has had to rule on tax issues, confirming that national laws must align with European principles. Generally, national tax laws must respect European regulations. However, when comparing international and European rules, international customary law prevails if the EU principles are not incorporated into international customary law. In particular, although business taxation remains a national competence (Artt. 113, 115 TFEU), it must nevertheless be exercised consistently with EU law (Schumaker, C-279/93, §21). On the other hand, taxpayers cannot enjoy freedom if, absent any valid commercial reasons, the sole purpose is reduction of tax (Cadbury Schweppes, C-196/04, §50). The EU may address distortions due to tax systems by (i) removing restrictions to exercise fundamental freedoms (Artt. 18, 21, 45, 49, 56, and 63 TFEU) and competition distortions (Artt. 101, 102, 106, 107, and 108 TFEU), or, alternatively by (ii) using two main procedures, being the infringement procedure ex Artt. 258–261 TFEU (when the EU Commission take legal action against Member States that fail to correctly implement EU law), or the procedure of State Aid control ex Art. 108 giving the EU Commission the power to take action against Member States also in tax measures.

In summary, the application of tax regulations depends on the perspective: if we consider the EU as a single entity, it must follow international rules, while if we look at individual Member States, they must respect European regulations when dealing with international law.

References

Avi-Yonah RS (2007) International tax as international law, Cambridge Tax Law Series. Cambridge University Press

Avi-Yonah RS (2019) Does customary international tax law exist? Law & Economics Working Papers 161

Braumann C (2020) Taxes and custom: tax treaties as evidence for customary international law. J Int Econ Law 23(3)

Broekhuijsen D, Valderrama IM (2021) Revisiting the case of customary international tax law. Int Community Law Rev 23

Paulson SL (1995) Radbruch on unjust laws: competing earlier and later views?, Oxford journal of legal studies, 15(3)

Tosi L, Baggio R (2023) International tax law in the Italian legal system, Cedam.

Chapter 13
International Tax Treaties

Contents

13.1 The OECD Model Tax Treaty

There are more than 3000 international tax treaties that aim to eliminate double taxation on income and capital by dividing the taxing powers between the State of residence and the State of source. Most of them are negotiated by referring to the Model Tax Convention (MTC) recommended by the Organization for Economic Co-operation and Development (OECD), although there are also other standards within the international tax community (i.e. the UN Model, the US Model and the Dutch Model).

The OECD Model Tax Convention serves as a fundamental framework for international tax treaties, aiming to streamline and clarify the complex landscape of cross-border taxation. At its core, the Convention includes several essential components that together create a cohesive structure for the interaction of tax systems from different countries.

In 1963, the OECD published the first Draft Model Double Taxation Convention on Income and Capital. This model introduced principles and definitions that remain central to tax treaties today, such as the concept of "permanent establishment" (PE) and rules for allocating taxing rights. While the draft was not legally binding, it served as a template for bilateral treaties and as a starting point for further refinement.

The 1977 release of the OECD Model Tax Convention marked its formal establishment as the primary reference for bilateral tax treaties. This version solidified key principles and introduced mechanisms for resolving disputes between countries

G. Marino, *The Dark Side of International Tax Law*,
https://doi.org/10.1007/978-3-032-08159-9_13

through a mutual agreement procedure (MAP). It also incorporated provisions addressing the prevention of tax evasion, reflecting growing concerns about abusive practices.

The 1977 Model was notable for its broad acceptance, shaping the tax treaty policies of OECD member states and influencing non-member countries. It balanced the competing interests of residence and source countries, albeit with a tilt toward the preferences of developed nations.

As global economic activities and business practices evolved, the OECD Model underwent periodic updates to address new challenges. A major consolidation occurred in 1992, accompanied by a detailed Commentary to enhance clarity and usability. Subsequent updates focus on (i) strengthening anti-abuse provisions to prevent treaty shopping; (ii) addressing the taxation of e-commerce and digital transactions; (iii) enhancing the transparency of cross-border tax arrangements through improved information exchange mechanisms and (iv) by the 2000s, the OECD Model had become an indispensable tool for countries navigating the complexities of globalization.

The OECD's Base Erosion and Profit Shifting (BEPS 1.0) Project, launched in 2013, marked a paradigm shift in international tax policy. The BEPS 1.0 initiative sought to counteract aggressive tax planning strategies that exploited gaps and mismatches in tax rules, leading to artificial profit shifting and the erosion of national tax bases.

The 2017 update to the OECD Model reflected many of the BEPS recommendations, introducing (i) a Principal Purpose Test (PPT) to prevent treaty abuse by denying benefits for transactions with no substantial economic purpose; (ii) revisions to the definition of "permanent establishment" to address artificial avoidance through fragmented activities or commissionaire arrangements and (iii) improved dispute resolution mechanisms, including mandatory binding arbitration for certain cases. These changes demonstrated the OECD's commitment to ensuring that tax treaties remain robust and fit for purpose in a rapidly changing economic landscape.

In the twenty-first century, the digitalization of the economy posed unprecedented challenges to traditional tax frameworks and tax treaties. Multinational enterprises (MNEs) with significant digital operations often escaped taxation in jurisdictions where they generated substantial revenues but had little physical presence.

The OECD's work culminated in the development of the Inclusive Framework on BEPS 2.0, which introduced two key pillars: (i) Pillar One: Reallocates taxing rights to market jurisdictions for large MNEs, ensuring a fairer distribution of profits; (ii) Pillar Two: Establishes a global minimum corporate tax rate of 15%, reducing incentives for profit shifting to low-tax jurisdictions.

The 2021 update to the OECD Model incorporated provisions to address these issues, signalling a new era of tax cooperation aimed at tackling the challenges of globalization and digitalization. Last but not least, on 18th November 2025, the OECD Council approved an update to the OECD MTC and its Commentary that modernises the MTC to reflect recent developments in global business and work, in particular, cross-border remote work and increased natural-resource activities.

The OECD Model Tax Convention has evolved significantly since its inception, adapting to the changing needs of the global economy while maintaining its core principles. From its origins in the League of Nations to its modern iterations addressing BEPS and digital taxation, the Model reflects an enduring commitment to fostering cooperation, preventing double taxation, and ensuring fair and effective taxation. As international tax challenges continue to evolve, the OECD Model remains a cornerstone of global tax policy, providing a framework for equitable and predictable cross-border taxation. Nevertheless, one may wonder whether its crisis of identity will last for one day.

1.1. Starting with the preamble (Chapter I), it sets the stage for the treaty, outlining the purpose and mutual intentions of the countries involved. This section helps to establish a collaborative spirit, emphasizing the importance of fair tax practices and cooperation.

Next, the definitions section (Chapter II) plays a crucial role in ensuring that all parties have a shared understanding of the terms used throughout the document. By defining key concepts, such as "resident" or "permanent establishment", the convention promotes consistency in interpretation and application.

The component detailing the substantive rules of taxation rights (Chapter III) is particularly significant. It delineates which country has the authority to tax specific types of income, such as income from immovable property, business profits, international shipping and air transportation, associated enterprises, dividends, interest, royalties, capital gains, income from employment, directors' fees, entertainers and sportspersons, pensions, government services, students and other income. This clarity is vital for preventing disputes over taxing rights, which can often lead to the double taxation of income earned by individuals and businesses operating in multiple jurisdictions.

A specific section is dedicated to the taxation of capital (Chapter V), represented by immovable or movable property, as well as the capital of enterprises represented by ships or aircraft.

To address the issue of double taxation directly, the Convention includes provisions for the elimination of double taxation (Chapter V). This section outlines methods, like exemptions or tax credits, that countries can apply to ensure that income is not taxed twice, providing a fairer environment for international trade and investment.

Furthermore, the procedural rules section (Chapter VI) is becoming of increasing importance since it contains the instruments of dialogue between the Tax Authorities of the Contracting States. First, the non-discrimination principle is designed to ensure that nationals of one Contracting State are not treated less favourably than nationals of the other Contracting State in similar circumstances. This principle is essential in promoting fairness and equity in international taxation, as it helps prevent discrimination that could arise from differential treatment based on nationality. Second, the mutual agreement procedure provides a mechanism for resolving disputes related to the interpretation or application of a treaty. This article is crucial for ensuring that taxpayers can seek relief from potential double taxation and other tax-related issues that arise from differing interpretations of tax laws by the Contracting States. Recently, it has been enriched by an arbitration procedure that gets closer to private dispute resolutions. Third, the exchange of information is designed to foster transparency and cooperation between Tax Authorities. By allowing countries to share relevant tax information, it acts as a deterrent against tax evasion and promotes compliance with international tax standards. The importance of the exchange of information is growing decade after decade; this is the reason why the contents of Article 26 have been shifted to other Models specifically dedicated to the matter, such as the Tax Information Exchange Agreement (TIEA) of 2002, the Convention on Mutual Administrative Assistance in Tax Matters (MAATM) of 1988 and the related Common Reporting Standards of 2014. Last, the assistance of tax collection typically refers to provisions in various tax treaties or agreements that facilitate cooperation between countries in tax matters. It aims to ensure that Tax Authorities can assist each other in enforcing tax laws, sharing information, and collecting taxes owed. This cooperation can help prevent tax evasion and ensure compliance with tax obligations, thereby enhancing the overall revenue collection for governments.

In recent years, the inclusion of anti-abuse provisions in the Model Tax Convention has become increasingly important. These measures are aimed at preventing tax avoidance strategies that exploit gaps or mismatches in tax rules, ensuring that the benefits of treaties are not misused.

Overall, the OECD Model Tax Convention offers a comprehensive and coherent structure that facilitates international cooperation in taxation while also addressing the complexities of modern tax challenges.

Chapter VII describes the final provisions, including entry into force and termination.

1.2. The OECD Model Tax Treaty is accompanied by a Commentary that plays a crucial but sometimes underappreciated role in the world of international tax. While the Model Tax Convention itself provides the framework for how two countries agree to divide taxing rights—for example, who can tax a company's profits or where an individual is considered a resident for tax purposes—the Commentary is what breathes life and clarity into the articles of the treaty.

Think of the Commentary as a detailed user manual that accompanies legal text. It explains what articles are meant to achieve, how key terms should be interpreted, and how provisions should be applied in practice. Without the Commentary, the treaty would often be too vague to deal with real-world tax complexities, especially in today's global economy, where multinational companies and cross-border investments are common.

Even though the Commentary is not legally binding, it carries significant authority. Many national courts, tax administrators and advisors turn to it for guidance when applying tax treaties. It's especially influential when both countries involved in a treaty are OECD members or have stated that their agreement is based on the OECD Model. In such cases, the Commentary reflects a shared understanding of what the treaty is supposed to mean.

Importantly, the Commentary also helps promote international consistency. Because tax treaties are negotiated between pairs of countries, there's always a risk that each one could interpret the rules differently. The Commentary acts as a common reference point, helping to align interpretations and avoid disputes—or at least resolve them more easily.

Over time, the Commentary has evolved. It is regularly updated to reflect changes in international tax norms, policy shifts, and new concerns like tax avoidance or digital business models. For example, in recent years, it has expanded to incorporate the outcomes of the OECD's BEPS project, which seeks to prevent multinational companies from exploiting loopholes to avoid paying taxes anywhere. Through these updates, the Commentary stays relevant and reflects current international standards.

Of course, the Commentary doesn't override the actual words of a treaty. If the treaty text is clear and specific, it takes precedence. In some legal systems, especially those that rely heavily on statutory interpretation, the Commentary may be considered less authoritative. Still, in practice, it remains one of the most respected and widely used tools in international tax law.

In essence, the OECD Commentary is not law, but it is law's closest advisor—shaping how tax treaties are read, applied, and understood around the world. This brings coherence to a global system built on bilateral agreements and helps countries, companies, and courts navigate the often-complex terrain of cross-border taxation.

13.2 The UN Model Tax Convention: History and Structure

International taxation plays a crucial role in facilitating cross-border trade, investment, and economic cooperation. The United Nations Model Double Taxation Convention between Developed and Developing Countries (commonly referred to as the UN Model Tax Convention) serves as a foundational guide for tax treaty negotiations between countries—particularly to ensure fairness between developed and developing nations. It provides a framework to allocate taxing rights and avoid double taxation while also limiting tax evasion and fostering international cooperation.

The development of the UN Model Tax Convention traces back to the post-World War II period, during which international organizations began to play an increasing role in shaping global economic policies. Here's a chronological overview of its evolution:

The foundation for modern model tax treaties was laid by the League of Nations in the 1920s and 1930s. The League's work recognized the challenges of double taxation and proposed solutions, including model treaties.

After World War II, the OECD developed a model tax convention—first released in 1963 and then updated periodically. However, many developing countries criticized it for favouring capital-exporting (mostly developed) countries by giving them greater taxing rights.

In response to these concerns, the United Nations took an active role. The UN Model Tax Convention was first released in 1980. Its goal was to strike a more equitable balance between the interests of source (often developing) and residential (usually developed) countries. It was drafted by the UN Group of Experts on Tax Treaties, composed of representatives from both developed and developing countries.

Subsequent revisions of the UN Model occurred in 2001, 2011, 2017 and 2021. This last revision aimed to address concerns expressed by developing countries regarding tax treaty obstacles to the taxation of foreign enterprises on income from automated digital services and gains from offshore indirect transfers. It also provided new guidance on the application and interpretation of the definition of permanent establishment, the concept of beneficial ownership, and the application of the Model's provisions to collective investment vehicles, pension funds, and real estate investment trusts.

In March 2025, the UN Tax Committee was expected to approve a revision to Article 8 of the Model Convention, which would introduce a choice between residence-based and source-based taxation for international air transport operators. This change aims to allow countries where airlines generate income to impose income taxes, potentially leading to enhanced state revenue in developing nations. However, this may also increase the risk of double taxation and add to administrative complexity.

Each edition reflects evolving international tax norms, emerging issues (e.g. digital economy, base erosion), and increased attention to tax transparency and anti-abuse provisions.

2.1. The UN Model Convention consists of two main parts: the Model Treaty text and Commentaries. The treaty follows a structured format that is largely like the OECD Model, with modifications tailored for developing countries. The structure includes:

a. Scope and Definitions (Articles 1–5)

- Article 1: Persons covered
- Article 2: Taxes covered
- Article 3–5: Definitions, including "residence" and "permanent establishment"

b. Allocation of Taxing Rights (Articles 6–22)

- Covers various categories of income and capital (e.g. income from immovable property, business profits, dividends, interest, royalties, capital gains, etc.)
- Key distinction: The UN Model allocates more taxing rights to the State of source compared to the OECD Model. For instance:
- Article 12 (Royalties): Unlike the OECD Model, the UN Model allows source-country taxation of royalties.
- Article 14 (Independent personal services): Retained in the UN Model (deleted from OECD), giving source countries more taxing power.

c. Elimination of Double Taxation (Article 23)

- Provides methods for residential countries to relieve double taxation, typically through tax credits or exemptions.

d. Non-Discrimination and Mutual Agreement Procedures (Articles 24–25)

- Ensures fair treatment and offers mechanisms to resolve tax disputes between states.

e. Exchange of Information and Administrative Cooperation (Articles 26–27)

- Encourages transparency and cooperation to combat tax evasion and avoidance.

f. Final Provisions (Articles 28–29)

- Address entry into force and termination procedures for the treaty.

Commentaries accompanying the UN Model are essential for understanding the intent and application of each article. They offer detailed explanations and examples, highlight differences from the OECD Model, and provide guidance on best practices for treaty interpretation and negotiation.

2.2. While both OECD and UN models aim to avoid double taxation and encourage international investment, key differences include (i) source-country bias, where the UN Model gives greater taxing rights to source countries, aligning with the interests of developing nations; (ii) broader permanent establishment rules, with a more expansive definition to ensure source countries can tax business profits arising within their territories (i.e. the shorter period of time an activity needs to qualify as PE in the State of source) and (iii) retained provisions for independent personal services and technical services, which are more relevant to developing economies.

The UN Model serves as a vital resource for developing countries in negotiating tax treaties that safeguard their tax rights and revenue bases. Though less widely used than the OECD Model, it influences many bilateral tax treaties involving developing countries and continues to evolve alongside global tax reforms.

Moreover, with increasing attention on tax justice, digital taxation, and base erosion and profit shifting (BEPS), the UN Model remains a crucial platform for representing the voices and concerns of less economically powerful states in global tax dialogues.

The UN Model Tax Convention embodies the United Nations' efforts to promote a more balanced international tax system that accounts for the needs of both developed and developing countries. While influenced by the OECD Model, it adopts key provisions to ensure equity, fairness, and sustainable tax revenues for source countries. As global tax systems continue to evolve, especially with initiatives like the OECD/G20 Inclusive Framework, the UN Model will likely continue to serve as a vital counterbalance and alternative reference point in international tax negotiations.

References

Avi-Yonah RS (2024) The first US tax treaty and its influence. Intertax 52(1)
Avi-Yonah RS, Mazzoni G (2021) Stanley Surrey, the 1981 US Model, and the Single Tax Principle. Intertax 49(8/9)
Brauner Y (2020) The true nature of tax treaties. Bull Int Tax 1
Brauner Y (2024) A UN dawn for the international tax regime. Intertax 52(2)
Danon RJ, Schoen W (2020) Foreword: tax treaty interpretation after BEPS. Bull Int Tax 4–5
Mason R (2004) US Tax Treaty Policy and the European Court of Justice. Tax Law Rev 58:2
Reimer E, Rust A (eds) (2022) Klaus Vogel on Double Taxation Conventions. Wolters Kluwer

Chapter 14
The BEPS Projects

Contents

14.1 The Framework of BEPS 1.0

The Base Erosion and Profit Shifting (BEPS) project was launched by the Organisation for Economic Co-operation and Development (OECD) in response to increasing concerns about tax avoidance strategies employed by multinational enterprises. These strategies allowed companies to shift profits from high-tax jurisdictions to low- or no-tax jurisdictions, resulting in significant revenue losses for governments worldwide. The initiative was largely influenced by the United States' need to recover from the financial crisis, leading it to push for a global framework to curb aggressive tax planning.

The BEPS project is structured around a master plan that consists of three fundamental pillars: (i) coherence—ensuring that international tax rules are consistent and eliminate mismatches that lead to double non-taxation; (ii) substance—ensuring that profits are taxed where economic activities generating them are performed and (iii) transparency and certainty—promoting information sharing among Tax Authorities and improving dispute resolution mechanisms.

These three pillars encompass 15 Actions, which address various aspects of international taxation and are designed to be implemented over different periods.

G. Marino, *The Dark Side of International Tax Law*,
https://doi.org/10.1007/978-3-032-08159-9_14

Action 1 preliminarily addresses the challenges posed by the digital economy, particularly the phenomenon of double non-taxation arising from digital transactions. Given the borderless nature of digital goods and services, traditional tax principles based on residential and source countries have become ineffective. The OECD advocates for a holistic approach that moves beyond physical presence to tackle taxation issues in a cloud-based economy.

14.2 The Coherence

Coherence in international tax rules prevents arbitrage opportunities that multinational enterprises exploit. This pillar includes the following actions: (i) hybrid mismatch arrangements (Action 2), where financial instruments often have different tax treatments in different jurisdictions. A common example involves an investment that is considered a dividend in the residence country (and thus tax-exempt under participation exemption rules) while simultaneously being treated as an interest expense in the source country (allowing a tax deduction). This results in double non-taxation. Coherence among countries ensures that such mismatches are minimized. (ii) Controlled foreign company (CFC) rules (Action 3), where CFC rules are designed to prevent profit shifting to low-tax jurisdictions. Currently, each country applies its CFC rules differently, leading to tax arbitrage. The OECD aims to harmonize these rules to prevent cherry-picking by multinational enterprises. (iii) Interest deduction limits (Action 4), in which countries must impose a cap on interest deductions to prevent excessive debt shifting. The goal is to establish a globally consistent 1:1 ratio of interest deductibility, ensuring fair capital structures across jurisdictions. (iv) harmful tax practices (Action 5), that is, the OECD's efforts to curb harmful tax practices date back to 1997. Nominal corporate tax rates can be misleading, as the effective tax burden may be significantly lower due to preferential tax regimes. Transparency measures ensure that parent companies are aware of the true tax liabilities of their subsidiaries.

14.3 The Substance

This substance ensures that profits are taxed where real economic activities occur. Key actions include (i) preventing Treaty Abuse (Action 6), which means treaties should not be exploited to achieve double non-taxation. The OECD model tax convention must be reinforced to prevent treaty shopping and (ii) avoid permanent establishment (PE) status (Action 7), which means that some companies fragment their operations to avoid PE status. For example, if a company separates its warehouse, workforce, and logistics into different legal entities, it may not trigger PE rules. The OECD seeks to close such loopholes to ensure that business presence is properly taxed; (iii) transfer pricing measures (Actions 8, 9 and 10), where these actions focus on ensuring that profits are allocated based on where value is truly created. Risks, capital allocation, and high-risk transactions should align with actual economic activities.

14.4 Transparency and Certainty

Transparency and Certainty foster cooperation among Tax Authorities and enhance legal certainty for businesses. The key actions include (i) measuring BEPS (Action 11), namely, countries must report BEPS-related tax data to the OECD to assess the project's effectiveness; (ii) disclosure rules (Action 12), where the European Union's Directive on Administrative Cooperation (6th Amendment, DAC6) directive is a key example of new reporting obligations requiring intermediaries to disclose aggressive tax arrangements and (iii) transfer pricing documentation (Action 13), that is, multinational enterprises must maintain standardized documentation, including a master file and country-specific reports. Today, Tax Administrations use cloud-based platforms to exchange this information, but concerns remain about governance and data control; (iv) dispute resolution (Action 14), where the OECD has improved dispute resolution mechanisms in tax treaties. If two Tax Administrations cannot agree, the process moves to arbitration, reducing the burden on taxpayers.

The Multilateral Instrument (Action 15) is a major challenge in implementing BEPS actions and ensuring global coordination. Instead of renegotiating thousands of bilateral treaties, Action 15 introduces a multilateral instrument (MLI) that allows countries to modify their treaties simultaneously. Once ratified, a country's existing treaties are automatically updated, creating a more efficient framework for international tax cooperation.

14.5 The Achievements of BEPS 1.0

Is BEPS representing a new tax order? It does not seem so since while the project aimed to tackle Base Erosion and Profit Shifting, the evolving economic landscape demands a shift toward another BEPS, being the Base Erosion and Profit Shifting. The digital economy, global mobility of capital, and new business models require continuous adaptation. Future reforms may focus on global minimum taxation, digital service taxes, and enhanced multilateral cooperation.

Specifically, consensus was not reached about taxing the digital economy (i.e. primarily the US and Chinese tech giants), transfer pricing was not reformed, and the PE threshold and arm's length standard remained in place despite both being obsolete in a digital economy context. In addition, relatively few of the BEPS 1.0 actions were minimum standards that had to be adopted by all participants.

Nevertheless, BEPS 1.0 represents a milestone in international tax policy, aiming to eliminate loopholes that enable tax avoidance while fostering fairness and efficiency in global taxation. Its success depends on consistent implementation and international cooperation. Moving forward, the challenge lies in balancing tax sovereignty with the need for a more integrated global tax system.

14.6 BEPS 1.0 Within the European Union

Recognizing the global significance of BEPS, the European Union decided to go a step further. While BEPS provides a common set of principles, its implementation is voluntary and varies from country to country. The European Union (EU) chose to transform key elements of the BEPS recommendations into binding law for its Member States through the Anti-Tax Avoidance Directive 2016/1164 of 12 July 2016, known as the Anti-Tax Avoidance Directive (ATAD). ATAD marked the EU's commitment not just to support the BEPS process but also to lead by example in enforcing uniform anti-avoidance rules within its own internal market.

ATAD transposes several core aspects of the BEPS Actions directly into EU legislation. This includes measures to limit excessive interest deductions, prevent the artificial shifting of profits to low-tax jurisdictions via controlled foreign companies, and impose taxation when assets are transferred out of the EU tax jurisdiction. It also introduces a general anti-abuse rule, empowering Tax Authorities to ignore arrangements that, although legal in form, are created solely to obtain a tax advantage. Later, ATAD 2 expanded the directive's scope by addressing hybrid mismatches—arrangements that exploit the differences between the two countries' tax systems to gain tax benefits.

What makes ATAD distinct from BEPS is its legal nature. While the BEPS framework relies on the voluntary cooperation of participating countries, ATAD is a directive—meaning all EU Member States are legally obliged to implement its provisions. This ensures consistency across the EU and prevents individual countries from becoming weak links in the fight against corporate tax avoidance.

At the same time, ATAD is not a carbon copy of BEPS. In some areas, this goes further than what the OECD has proposed. In others, it adapts BEPS measures to reflect the EU's own legal principles and the specific needs of the internal market. Therefore, the relationship between the two initiatives is complementary. BEPS sets the global standard, and ATAD builds on it, turning recommendations into enforceable rules within Europe.

Ultimately, both ATAD and BEPS reflect a growing international consensus that tax systems need to catch up with globalization. As companies operate across borders with ease, Tax Authorities must also work across borders to ensure profits are taxed where real economic activity takes place. While still work remains, the coordinated action represented by BEPS and ATAD shows that reform is not only possible but already underway—and that international tax rules can evolve to be both fairer and more effective in the face of twenty-first century challenges.

14.7 BEPS 2.0

It became increasingly clear that the rules needed to change. Companies like tech platforms, streaming services, and online retailers earn massive revenues from users in countries where they have no physical presence. Under existing tax rules, these countries were often powerless to tax such profits and reacted by adopting digital services taxes (DSTs) and equalization levies (ELs) designed to bypass tax treaty limits in taxing the digital economy. The result was a growing sense of imbalance between developed and developing countries, between digital and brick-and-mortar businesses, and between those who paid taxes and those who found ways not to or simply did not pay due to their innovative business.

The international political pressure brought to BEPS 2.0 consists of a two-pillar solution designed to modernize the international tax system and address the tax challenges of digitalization.

Pillar One represents a radical shift. It proposes to allocate a portion of the profits of the largest multinational enterprises to the countries where their consumers or users are located, regardless of whether the company has a physical presence there. This is a major departure from the old rules, which required a company to have a fixed place of business—a permanent establishment—before profits could be taxed. With Pillar One, tax rights follow the market, not the infrastructure. The goal is to ensure that the values created by user participation and digital engagement are reflected in the allocation of tax rights.

Pillar Two, meanwhile, focuses on ensuring that multinational companies—no matter where they operate—pay a minimum level of tax. Known as the Global Minimum Tax (GMT), this measure would establish a floor on corporate taxation, set at 15%. If a company pays less than this rate in a low-tax country, other countries where it operates would be allowed to "top up" the tax, eliminating the benefit of shifting profits to tax havens. A sort of "prisoner's dilemma game". The purpose is to prevent a race to the bottom in corporate tax rates and safeguard the tax bases of countries around the world.

These two pillars are not just theoretical ideas. In October 2021, after years of negotiations, over 135 countries and jurisdictions—representing more than 90% of global Gross Domestic Product (GDP)—agreed to the broad outlines of the BEPS 2.0 reforms. This political agreement marked a historic moment in international cooperation, one that promises to reshape the tax environment of the world's largest companies.

Still, the path from agreement to implementation is yet to be determined. Turning high-level political consensus into binding law requires legislative action at the national level, coordination among Tax Authorities, detailed technical complex work and, ironically enough, more software programs to manage GMT. Several countries have already begun the process of incorporating GMT into their domestic laws, while international bodies like the OECD are still working to finalize the mechanisms for profit reallocation under Pillar One. But resistance remains in some quarters, particularly from countries concerned about losing tax sovereignty or the administrative burdens involved, with the United States at the top of the list.

Within this scenario, the European Union courageously (or irresponsibly ?) anticipated GMT through Directive 2022/2523 of 15 December 2022, which entered into force on 1 January 2023 with the scope to adapt the GMT architecture to EU principles such as subsidiarity, proportionality, legal certainty, non-discrimination, and respect for national tax sovereignty, all while ensuring the smooth functioning of the internal market. This careful alignment was essential for the directive's legal legitimacy and political acceptability across all EU Member States.

Despite these challenges, BEPS 2.0 represents a watershed moment. It acknowledges that economic value is no longer confined to factories and offices and that tax systems must evolve in a world where companies can reach millions of customers without ever setting foot in their countries. More broadly, it reflects a renewed commitment to multilateralism—the idea that in an interconnected world, no single country can tackle global tax avoidance alone.

Whether BEPS 2.0 will deliver on its promise depends on how fully and faithfully the countries implement it. But one thing is clear: the foundations of international taxation are being reimagined, and the era of tax rules built for a brick-and-mortar economy is giving way to one more attuned to the realities of the digital age.

References

Avi-Yonah RS (2022) International taxation, globalization, and the economic digital divide. U of Michigan Public Law Research Paper n. 22-040

Chukwudumogu C (2024) Inter-nation equity and the regulation of tax competition via the global minimum tax rule: a case for improvement. Intertax 52(10)

David Rosenbloom H, Brothers JP (2015) Reflections on the intersection of U.S. tax treaty policy, U.S. tax reform, and BEPS. Tax Notes Int 78(8)

Dowd T, Landefeld P, Moore A (2017) Profit shifting of U.S. multinationals. J Public Econ 148

Kofler G (2021-2) The future of digital services taxes. EC Tax Review

Kysar RM (2024) The global tax deal and the new international economic governance. Tax Law Rev 77:2

OECD (2013) Action plan on base erosion and profit shifting. Paris

OECD (2019) Public Consultation Document: Global Anti-Base Erosion Proposal ("GloBE"). Paris

Schoen W (2020) Interpreting European Law in the Light of the OECD/G20 Base Erosion and Profit Shifting Action Plan. Bull Int Tax 4–5

Schoen W (2021) Is there finally an international tax system? World Tax J 13(3)

Torslov TR, Wier LS, Zucman G (2020) The missing profits of nations. National Bureau of Economic Research, April 2020

Chapter 15
Selected Topics of International Taxation

Contents

15.1 The World of Tax Havens

Tax havens have to do with passive income and inspire mixed feelings. They violate any morals when associated with money laundering of criminal economies, financing of international terrorism and tax fraud. They hypnotize when associated with the beauty of the places that distinguish them, the movies of James Bond that describe them and the treasures and secrets that they protect.

Throughout history, tax havens have been opposed at various stages by the most industrialized countries and their international organizations, as President Kennedy did in 1961, and as the G8 (now G7), G20, the OECD and the FATF (Financial Action Task Force—Groupe d'Action Financière) have since 1998.

G. Marino, *The Dark Side of International Tax Law*,
https://doi.org/10.1007/978-3-032-08159-9_15

But they are also tolerated, if not even used, in an almost love-hate relationship. They have a chameleon-like appearance because they can sometimes be tax havens, banking havens with secrecy, corporate havens with anonymous corporate vehicles, or even criminal havens.

But where are they?

Once upon a time, spread across the various continents and with different histories behind them, there were free trade marketplaces that specialized in offering tax-free services to individuals, for example, Tangier in Morocco, Beirut in the Middle East, together with Dubai, Panama in Central America, Uruguay in South America, islands like the Bahamas and the Netherlands. Antilles in the Caribbean, Hong Kong and Singapore in the Far East, Liechtenstein, Monaco and the United Kingdom in Europe, and at the very top of this League, there was certainly Switzerland. Never in Italy, unfortunately, despite the beauty of many islands like the astonishing Aeolians with the beloved Salina. Other countries have emerged over the decades for tax-free services rendered to multinational corporations in Europe, such as Luxembourg and the Netherlands.

With the age of cooperation that started in 1998, it is no longer possible to picture a country as a tax haven, since many countries have peculiar provisions within their tax legislation that make them a tax haven for specific purposes. It is a strange feeling to face a country being recognizable as a tax inferno for most taxpayers that suddenly becomes a tax haven for a few clients, generally foreign high-net-worth individuals or multinational enterprises. As an example of this new trend, Italy can be mentioned for its brand new resident non-domiciled status as well as for its very low inheritance and succession tax (that reminds the saying "see Naples and then die"), which in turn the UK has eliminated after Brexit, and the United States for refusing to exchange its own tax information with other countries.

1.1. While in the past classic tax havens could have only been imagined through books and movies, only with the famous tax whistleblower's public opinion and Institutions discovered in their full magnitude.

While whistleblowing belongs to ancient history and includes famous examples of the subject, such as Judas Iscariot, who sold Jesus Christ for 30 pieces of silver, it is above all contemporary history that offers the most emblematic cases in which public opinion has reacted to such an extent that it has made the intervention of legislative power necessary. It is no coincidence that most of these affairs, reported by the media as scandals, occurred when science and digital technology began their predominance, by virtue of which the change in tools determines the change in purpose. A breach of privacy with big data is always around the corner.

Five of them will be examined in chronological order, starting with the scandal of the LGT bank of Liechtenstein up to the most recent Panama Papers investigation, on which the irony of capitalism, Netflix, an icon of the tax-free digital economy, has also produced a film.

Heinrich Kieber, a computer technician by profession, was commissioned by the LGT of the Principality of Liechtenstein to digitize the bank's paper archive, and in doing so he thought it was a good idea to pour the data of clients, mainly European and Russian, into DVDs that he sold to the German secret service for 6 million euros (subject to taxation in Germany with a withholding tax of 30%). The theft of the data dates to 2002, while the scandal dates to 2008 and affected German public opinion, inducing the president of the Deutsche Post, Klaus Zumwinkel, included in the list for an undeclared account of 1 million euros, to immediately resign. In Italy, too, the list was the subject of media dissemination and investigations by the Revenue and various Public Prosecutors' Offices. Heinrich Kieber was tried in absentia by the Principality Authorities, published his memoirs and appears to have taken refuge in Australia under a cover identity provided by the Germans.

While the LGT scandal was breaking out in 2008, another one of bigger proportions was being created by Bradley C. Birkenfeld, an American banker at the Geneva branch of the UBS, in retaliation against the Swiss bank, which he believed was guilty of having tacitly introduced recommendations within the bank on how to manage American clients after the Obama Administration's declarations of war on tax havens, keeping the bankers directly involved in the dark so as to continue earning large commissions but distance the bank in the event of a scandal. By downloading thousands of data delivered to the American Authorities, Bradley Birkenfeld joined the tax whistleblowing programme that allowed the Internal Revenue Service to recover over 15 billion dollars embezzled from taxes. He collected a (gross) prize of 104 million dollars that he was able to enjoy only after serving 30 months in a federal prison, requested and obtained by the Department of Justice for complicity in international tax evasion and fraud together with the bank, which in turn was fined 780 million dollars.

More romantic is the story of Hervè Falciani, an Italian engineer naturalized in France who in 2010 stole, through downloading data from 130,000 current accounts attributable to 80,000 clients from 180 countries of the Swiss branch of the HSBC bank, a part of which made up the "Lagarde list" (as it was sent to the then French Minister of the Treasury Christine Lagarde), while the Italian portion is known as the "Falciani list". Falciani's declared goal was not to make a profit from his transparent reporting but rather to help spread the culture of fulfilling tax obligations at an international level. In 2015, the Court of Bellinzona sentenced him in absentia to 5 years of imprisonment for economic espionage, while in 2019, the bank was sentenced in France and Belgium to a fine of over 350 million euros for aiding and abetting international tax evasion and fraud.

Also in 2010, the French professional Antoine Deltour of the Luxembourg branch of the audit firm PwC accessed the company's automated data processing system to steal the tax agreements concluded between PwC and the Luxembourg Tax Authorities on behalf of PwC corporate clients and handed them over to journalist Edouard Perrin, who, through the International Consortium of Investigative Journalists (ICJI), in 2014 amplified the incident that gave rise to the LuxLeaks scandal, to the deep embarrassment of the then new President of the European Commission Jean-Claude Juncker, who at the time of the events was Prime Minister of the Grand Duchy. Antoine Deltour, first convicted of national theft of documents, fraudulent access to the automated system, disclosure of the employer's business secrets, violation of professional secrecy and money laundering through possession and use, with knowledge of their fraudulent origin, of the same documents, was then acquitted based on the justification derived from his status as an informer.

Finally, the Panama Papers scandal, named after a confidential file, was digitized and composed of 11.5 million confidential documents for over 2.6 terabytes, stolen by a deep throat (conventionally identified with the name of John Doe) of the Panamanian law firm Mossak and Fonseca. This file provides detailed information from the seventies on over 214,000 offshore companies, including the identities of shareholders, entrepreneurs, artists and sportsmen, political leaders, public officials, close collaborators and their relatives from over 40 countries.

The collection was delivered to the newspaper Süddeutsche Zeitung in August 2015 and subsequently to the International Consortium of Investigative Journalists (ICIJ) via encrypted formats and email. The files were distributed and analysed by approximately 400 journalists from 107 news organizations in over 80 countries. The first report based on the set of documents was published, together with 149 of the documents themselves, on 3 April 2016. Due to the unprecedented scale and gravity of the phenomenon, the European Parliament decided in June 2016 to establish a Commission of Inquiry composed of 65 MEPs with the task of investigating alleged violations and cases of non-compliance by the Commission or the Member States with European rules on money laundering, tax avoidance and tax evasion.

In 2019, even Netflix produced a film about it with important actors, and the curiosity to know if, during their life as taxpayers or friends of taxpayers, they were directly interested in the story would never be satisfied.

Of course, all these episodes are those that, due to their digital and media dimensions, have taken on a historic clamour, but there are many others, and there will be, under the tips of these icebergs. For example, the Paradise Papers leak of 2017 contained around 13.4 million files, most of which came from Appleby, a prestigious offshore law firm based in Bermuda, and Asiaciti Trust, a wealth management firm based in Singapore. The files were obtained by the German newspaper Süddeutsche Zeitung and shared with the International Consortium of Investigative Journalists (ICIJ), who worked with hundreds of journalists worldwide to analyse and publish the findings.

What deserves to be emphasized is that such empirical evidence may also be the result of illicit conduct by the protagonists themselves (all foreigners with respect to their employer and still degraded to the rank of spies or informers), but the moral pressure that they were able to promote in public opinion, each with their own ethical justifications, was such as to lead to the legal overcoming of their behaviour as illicit, to the point of transforming them into legal whistleblowers.

15.2 The Modern War Against the Offshore World: The Exchange of Information

Several issues were already clear at the beginning of the twenty-first century. The globalization of business has considerably raised the number of tax-relevant cross-border transactions, as well as considerably increased the mobility of taxpayers moving from one country to another and of their capital, which is more often shifted offshore. The 2008 financial crisis brought clear statements by the Group of Eight (G8, now G7) and Group of Twenty (G20) in favour of fighting international tax fraud and securing tax revenue: a milestone was the G20 statement at the London summit in April 2009 in order to intensify the pressure on tax havens by publishing a list of tax havens that are not compliant. Furthermore, the package of measures to stabilise the world economy and financial markets agreed upon at the G20 Finance Ministers meeting at the beginning of September 2009 also included the fight against uncooperative behaviour regarding the exchange of information in tax matters. The need for academic comment and reflection was great at that time since neither national literature on mutual assistance and information exchange in tax matters nor a Europe-wide comparison was available. Four levels of legal bases were identified: (i) the European level, (ii) multilateral agreements, (iii) bilateral agreements and (iv) unilateral rules regulating administrative assistance in tax matters.

On 20 July 2013 the G20 Finance Ministers and Central Bank Governors endorsed the OECD proposals for a global model of automatic exchange of information (AEOI) in the multilateral context. On 6 September 2013 the G20 leaders reinforced this message and said, "Calling on all other jurisdictions to join us by the earliest possible date, we are committed to automatic exchange of information as the new global standard, which must ensure confidentiality and the proper use of information exchanged, and we fully support the OECD work with G20 countries aimed at presenting such a single global standard for automatic exchange by February 2014 and to finalizing technical modalities of effective automatic exchange by mid-2014". They also asked the Global Forum on Transparency and Exchange of Information for Tax Purposes of the OECD to establish a mechanism to monitor and review the implementation of a new global standard for the automatic exchange of information and stressed the importance of developing countries being able to benefit from a more transparent international tax system.

2013 is behind the corner, but it looks like a century ago in this field, so another way to study this topic is to describe the present time. In this respect, first, the feeling is that today the definition "mutual assistance" is leaving the floor to the more stringent single term "cooperation". The Foreign Account Tax Compliance Act (FATCA), which was aimed at ensuring that the US Internal Revenue Service could identify and collect the appropriate tax from US persons holding financial assets outside the United States, is now a cooperative tool in the hands of many European States to stay in the wave of getting from the rest of the world as much automatic information as possible on their own resident taxpayers from foreign financial institutions (FFIs).

2.1. With the incredible exception of the United States, as of early 2025, 120 jurisdictions have committed to the automatic exchange of information (AEOI) provided by the Global Forum. This commitment is part of the global effort to combat tax evasion and avoidance. The common reporting standard (CRS) facilitates the exchange of financial account information between Tax Authorities, enhancing transparency and cooperation in tax matters. These jurisdictions include a diverse range of countries and territories, encompassing major financial centres, developing nations and offshore jurisdictions. The implementation of CRS is overseen by the OECD's Global Forum on Transparency and Exchange of Information for Tax Purposes, which monitors compliance and provides technical assistance to member countries.

The widespread adoption of CRS underscores the global consensus on the importance of transparency and the need for coordinated efforts to address cross-border tax issues. This initiative has led to the establishment of over 5400 bilateral exchange relationships, significantly increasing the volume of financial information exchanged among Tax Authorities.

What kind of automatic information, or better, how deep the automatic information should be, is of course the question mark, and the clear feeling on this matter is that the anti-money laundering and financing terrorism legislation approach to "know-your-client" (AML/KYC) is overriding any imputation of income and assets according to traditional tax law principles. At the same time, nevertheless, as demonstrated already by the 2010 comparative analysis, guidance and policy advice of the OECD on offshore voluntary disclosure programmes put in place by each single country playing in the international tax chessboard, unilateral mechanisms are always taken into account to enable non-compliant taxpayers to declare income and wealth that they have kept secret in the past by means of taking advantage of strict bank secrecy jurisdictions. When voluntary disclosures and/or whistleblower programmes are exhausted, then bilateral initiatives take place, like the Rubik-style agreements that Switzerland and Liechtenstein have negotiated with several European countries. All these issues are officially included in the tax policy agenda of international organizations (OECD), supranational bodies (EU) and single States. Again, tax policies seem to melt medium- to long-term sticks with short-term carrots.

15.3 The Sources of the Exchange of Information System at the International Level

As anticipated above, there is a matrix of legal platforms involved with the exchange of information, whether national, international or European, with an extraordinary explosion of legal instruments dealing with the exchange of information. In theory, this gives rise to hierarchies, competition and overlapping, which need to be analysed and solved. In practice, the effective use of these legal instruments must be understood with the aim of sharing information with the idea of reaching their simplification.

3.1. As far as the international legal base is concerned, exchange of information comes in different forms and includes exchange upon request, spontaneous information exchange and automatic exchange of information. The OECD has a long history of working on all forms of information exchange. Article 26 of the OECD Model Tax Convention (MTC) provides a basis for all three forms of information exchange with the scope to cover all tax matters without prejudice to the general rules and legal provisions governing the rights of defendants and witnesses in judicial proceedings. The OECD's work on exchange upon request and the more recent peer review work of the Global Forum on Transparency and Exchange of Information are well known. Based on these works, Article 26 of the OECD MTC was first updated in July 2005, when paragraphs 4 and 5 were added. They now make clear that a State cannot refuse a request for information solely because it has no domestic tax interest in the information (paragraph 4) or solely because it is held by a bank or other financial institution, nominee, or person acting in an agency or a fiduciary capacity, or because it relates to ownership interest in a person (paragraph 5). Then, in July 2012, an amendment to paragraph 2 specified that information received by a Contracting State may be used for other purposes (for example, may be remitted by the Tax Authorities to other law enforcement Agencies and judicial Authorities for high-priority matters like money laundering, corruption and terrorism financing) when such information may be used for other purposes under the laws of both States and the competent authority of the supplying State authorizes such use. At the same time, the Commentary was updated regarding the interpretation of the standard of "foreseeable relevance" and the term "fishing expeditions" with respect to a group of taxpayers not individually identified. An example of how fishing expeditions could work in the future comes from the decision of 11 September 2016 of the Swiss Federal Supreme Court, which ruled in favour of a request from the Netherlands for information on Dutch account holders at Swiss banks without names, making use of the double taxation convention agreement, which must ensure a broad exchange of information.

3.2. Meanwhile, the OECD has been continuing to develop instruments which provide a legal framework for the exchange of information, a charming one being the Tax Information Exchange Agreement (TIEA) of 2002, which gave a boost to relationships with non-cooperative countries as of 2009, when the London G20 summit of 2 April 2009 imposed on them at least 12 TIEAs with member countries in order to appear on the white list. Just like Article 26(1) of the OECD Model, Article 5(1) of the OECD TIEA provides information exchange for both civil and criminal tax matters, irrespective of whether the conduct being investigated would also constitute a crime under the laws of the requested party. In June 2015, the OECD Committee on Fiscal Affairs (CFA) approved a Modern Protocol for the Agreement, which may be used by jurisdictions in case they want to extend the scope of existing TIEAs to also cover the AEOI and/or spontaneous exchange of information. By June 2013, over 800 TIEAs had been signed, and among European countries, the longest lists, with more than 30 TIEAs, belong to Finland, France, Germany, the Netherlands, Sweden, as well as to the United States. It is worth noting the policy followed by Nordic countries (Denmark, the Faroe Islands and Greenland, Finland, Iceland, Norway and Sweden) of recognizing each other's

TIEA successfully negotiated by one of them with a tax haven. The impression is that although the OECD considers the signing of TIEAs a key policy instrument in the fight against tax evasion, there is little evidence about their quality, quantity and effectiveness.

3.3. A strange destiny is related to the Multilateral Convention on Mutual Administrative Assistance in Tax Matters (OECD Multilateral Convention on MAATM) put forward by the OECD in cooperation with the Council of Europe, which opened for signature by member states of both organizations on 25 January 1988. The Convention is the most comprehensive multilateral instrument available for all forms of tax cooperation to tackle tax evasion and avoidance and is a top priority for all countries. This sleeping beauty was amended on 31 March 2010 to respond to the call of the G20 at its April 2009 London summit to align it with the international standard on exchange of information upon request and to open it to all countries, to ensure that developing countries could benefit from the new, more transparent environment. Since then, the G20 has consistently encouraged countries to sign the Convention. However, its media turnaround was when Switzerland signed it with no reservation on 15 October 2013 and deposited it on 26 September 2016 through its Ambassador at the OECD, Ulrich Lehner, the instrument of ratification with entry into force on 1 January 2017. Currently, 140 jurisdictions have signed or committed to the Convention. With the incredible exception of the United States, the Convention collects a wide range of countries, including all G20 countries, all BRICS countries, almost all OECD countries, major financial centres and a growing number of developing countries. The Convention has taken on increasing importance with the G20's call for the automatic exchange of information (AEOI) to become the new international tax standard of exchange of information. Strange but true, the Convention, by virtue of its Article 6, requires the Competent Authorities of the Parties to the Convention to mutually agree on the scope of AEOI and the procedure to be complied with. With that background, the OECD approved on 15 July 2014 a Common Reporting Standard (CRS) which is based on (i) a model Competent Authority Agreement (CAA) providing the international legal framework for the automatic exchange of CRS information, (ii) the CRS, (iii) the Commentaries on CAA and CRS and (iv) the CRS XML schema user guide.

3.4. While the Multilateral Convention on MAATM sounds more adequate for de-offshoring the wealth of private individuals, as far as corporations are concerned, the Base Erosion Profit Shifting (BEPS) Action Plan adopted by the OECD and G20 countries in 2013 recognized that enhancing transparency for Tax Administrations by providing them with adequate information to assess high-level transfer pricing and other BEPS-related risks is a crucial aspect for tackling the BEPS problem. Specifically, the BEPS Action 13 Report provides a template for multinational enterprises (MNEs) to report annually, and for each tax jurisdiction in which they do business, the information set out therein. This Report is called the Country-by-Country (CbC) Report.

3.5. Finally, the Global Forum on Transparency and Exchange of Information for Tax Purposes was profoundly restructured in 2009 following the call from the G20 to ensure rapid implementation of the standards through the establishment of a rigorous and comprehensive peer review process in two steps. Today, the Global Forum exercises more than moral suasion against participating countries through due diligence. During the first phase, an examination is conducted to check whether the legal instruments for the exchange of information are in place or if they are just a collection. The second phase focuses on checking the effectiveness and efficiency of the exchange of information. The analysis of the offshore centre reports on this issue supports the feeling that this due diligence has created conditions to accelerate many domestic changes in the field.

15.4 At the Origin of the Automatic Exchange of Information: The FATCA

There are many reasons behind the rise of the Foreign Account Tax Compliance Act (FATCA), and there are many reasons behind the supremacy of FATCA over similar initiatives of automatic exchange of information. Starting in 2001, the United States has undertaken a series of aggressive tax enforcements, the first being the "Qualified Intermediary" (QI) agreements, where foreign financial institutions (FFIs) had to determine the identity of their clients other than non-US clients, including corporations, trusts and other entities. However, the 2008 highly publicized whistleblower case of Bradley Birkenfeld, a former banker at UBS, and the IRS's related John Doe summonses revealed that financial institutions encouraged US taxpayers to form foreign shell entities to open offshore accounts, bypassing the QI duties. The Congress enacted FATCA in 2010 in response to the weaknesses of the QI regime leading to the offshore evasion epidemic and the budgetary need to fund the controversial Obama's healthcare reform. In essence, FFIs and foreign financial entities must agree to disclose information on US account holders, or they become subject to a 30 per cent withholding tax payment on any transfer made to them out of the United States. FATCA has been characterized as "aggressive", "audacious", "egregious", "draconian" and "devastatingly destructive". It is not only unilateral but also extraterritorial since it requires FFIs to act like "US Treasury watchdogs" with billions of dollars in implementation costs. In a single message, FATCA will not survive. This prophecy seems to have been discharged by the OECD, which in 2012 delivered to the G20 the report "Automatic Exchange of Information: What it is, how it works, Benefits, what remains to be done", which summarizes the key features of an effective model for automatic exchange. The main success factors for the effective automatic exchange of financial information are 1) a common standard on information reporting, due diligence, and exchange of information; 2) a legal and operational basis for the exchange of information and 3) common or compatible technical solutions.

4.1. However, strange enough, the supremacy of FATCA over similar initiatives of AEOI seems to have more European than American origins, since it is largely related to the assumption of 5 European countries (France, Germany, Italy, Spain and the UK, known as the G5) that the US revolutionary scheme has the virtue to enhance multilateral cooperation in combating tax evasion but the vice to disclose information protected under European and domestic law to the IRS. On 8 February 2012, a Joint Statement was issued by the G5 with the United States, stating the intergovernmental approach to be developed in close cooperation with other partner countries, the OECD and, when appropriate, the EU Commission, towards common reporting and due diligence standards in support of a more global approach to effectively combating tax evasion while minimizing the compliance burden. The Joint Statement changed the unilateral nature of FATCA, which will become an instrument for US bilateral AEOI, forwarding to multilateralism. The related Model Agreement to Improve Tax Compliance and Implement FATCA was published on 26 July 2012. It simplifies administrative procedures so that FFIs will provide the respective foreign governments with the required information, and the respective governments will provide that information to the US government. It would reduce the original estimated compliance costs of USD 50–100 million per FFI, although according to recent literature, the upfront costs for the major banks equal expected revenue for the first ten years. If the ongoing costs for financial institutions and the cost of administration for the IRS and foreign tax authorities are included (insofar as they are known), the total costs are expected to exceed the revenue to be raised. On the other hand, data protection issues are far from being solved, since it is not clear to what extent the US will agree to provide reciprocal information to foreign countries. On 9 April 2013, the Ministers of Finance of France, Germany, Italy, Spain and the UK announced their intention to exchange FATCA-type information amongst themselves in addition to exchanging information with the United States. On 13 April 2013, Belgium, the Czech Republic, the Netherlands, Poland and Romania also expressed interest in this approach, which by 14 May 2013, had already been endorsed by 17 countries, with Mexico and Norway joining the initiative in early June and Australia in July.

4.2. There are 2 FATCA model intergovernmental agreements (IGAs): 1) IGA 1, negotiated with G5, provides that FFIs report certain financial account information to their respective tax authorities, who share the information with the IRS through AEOI under existing bilateral tax treaties or TIEAs. There are 3 versions of IGA 1: (i) a reciprocal version, (ii) a non-reciprocal version where there is a pre-existing ITC or TIEA and (iii) a non-reciprocal version where there is no pre-existing ITC or TIEA. The reciprocal version of the model also provides for the United States to exchange information currently collected on accounts held in US FIs by residents of partner countries and includes a policy commitment to pursue regulations and support legislation that would provide for equivalent levels of exchange by the US (however, the reciprocal version is never reciprocal, since the United States requires information but does not give back the same quality of information). This version of the model agreement will be available only to jurisdictions with which the US has in effect an ITC or TIEA and with respect to whom the Treasury Department and the IRS have determined that the recipient government has in place robust protections and practices to ensure that the information remains and is used solely for tax purposes. The US will make this decision on a case-by-case basis. Finally, 2) IGA 2 provides that FFIs report directly to the IRS. There are two versions of IGA 2: one for a pre-existing ITC or TIEA, and one where no such arrangements are in place.

4.3. Since the publication of the Model Agreement to Improve Tax Compliance and Implement FATCA on 26 July 2012, the number of countries signing up to the G5 Model rapidly increased (more than 110 jurisdictions, including Luxembourg, Liechtenstein, Colombia, Greece, Iceland and Malta, excluding Russia, whose agreement at this stage could only be achieved by means of a new Protocol to the US/Russia tax treaty), confirming the evolution of FATCA from unilateralism to multilateralism. At the same time, it is worth noting the adoption of FATCA-like legislation or treaties by other jurisdictions. For example, the UK implemented the "sons of FATCA" signed with several of its Crown Dependencies (Isle of Man, Guernsey, and Jersey) and Overseas Territories (Anguilla, Cayman Islands, Bermuda, Montserrat, Turks and Caicos, Gibraltar and the British Virgin Islands), while in the same vein, France studies a "mini-FATCA".

4.4. The legitimacy doubts of FATCA, that is, its administrative nature and its intrusive potentiality in taxpayers' privacy without legislative consent, seem to emerge from many perspectives. There is sensitivity to the issues of FFIs' FATCA implementation costs and the data protection rights of the taxpayer, since it is not yet clear how domestic legislation will be adequately amended to take care of FFIs'/tax administrations' FATCA obligations. Unless FFIs have a specific clause in terms of the business they have signed with their existing clients, it is not possible to hand over information to the IRS, insofar as Directive 95/46/EC bars transferring personal data to other entities without the explicit consent of the data subject. If an FFI breaches a contract without a contractual right, then they run the risk of legal action by the client for reinstatement of the contract and damages and sanctions by regulators.

4.5. Finally, it must be mentioned that probably the most intrusive instrument of exchange of information is the Swift Brussels Agreement, which was formalized in late 2009 and provides the Central Intelligence Agency (CIA) with powers to access bank accounts held by individuals in the European Union. The Brussels agreement requires that all 27 Member States grant requests of the CIA for banking information "as a matter of urgency" under the terrorist finance tracking programme. The banking records are to be kept for five years in a CIA database in Langley, Virginia, and it is not clear whether they may be passed on to other Authorities in the United States, such as the Federal Bureau of Investigation (FBI) and the Internal Revenue Service. One of the reasons for rushing through the Brussels agreement was the fact that Swift, at the end of 2009, moved part of its systems infrastructure and business operations to Switzerland, away from existing computing bases in Brussels and the

United States. This placed significant amounts of data outside the EU and US jurisdictions, a change apparently demanded by Swiss banks and others concerned with the privacy of their clients' information. Several banks had threatened to stop using the SWIFT system if additional privacy protection was not put in place.

15.5 The Automatic Exchange of Tax Information (AEOI) Under EU Law

The "big bang" at the European level is represented by the adoption of Council Directive 2011/16/EU of 15 February 2011, on "administrative cooperation in the field of taxation and repealing Directive 77/799/EEC" (hereinafter DAC), whose aim is to propose a new approach to overcome the negative effects of an ever-increasing globalization on the internal market. It is worth noting that the DAC makes reference to an "administrative cooperation" in the field of taxation, which is coherent with Article 197 of the Treaty on the Functioning of the European Union, while the repealed Directive 77/799/EEC was only concerning a "mutual assistance" by the Competent Authorities of the Member States in the field of direct taxation, which had consequences in terms of inefficiency and delays in communication, as if there were Chinese walls among Tax Administrations. The hope for more direct contact between Member States' local or national Tax Offices, with communication between central liaison offices being the rule, is well explained in Preamble n. 8 and has an intrinsic value going beyond any technical improvement introduced by the new Directive. It is indeed obvious that language skills, standardized electronic forms, clear office responses and the real practice of reciprocity are important human and administrative preconditions for any effective cross-border tax relationship. To this extent, while at the present time "administrative cooperation" is the right terminology to solve the described negative mood of the "mutual assistance", the future terminology to solve the possible obsolescence of this Directive will likely be "administrative integration". So far, from "mutual assistance" to "administrative integration", passing through "administrative cooperation". It could be proved that the integration of European tax systems is moving more through the level playing field of managing taxes than through the level playing field of their architecture (i.e. the common consolidated corporate base taxation (CCCTB) project).

5.1. DAC is revolutionary in many aspects. First, it is designed to follow a more intrusive mechanism for the collection of tax information other than VAT, custom and excise duties, allowing rules that make it possible to cover all legal and natural persons in the European Union, taking into account the ever-increasing range of legal arrangements, including not only the traditional arrangements such as trusts, foundations and investment funds, but also any new instruments that may be set up by taxpayers in the Member States (Article 3). Second, Member States could not refuse to transmit information because they have no domestic interest or because the information is held by a bank, any other financial institution, nominee or person acting in an agency or fiduciary capacity or because it relates to ownership interests in a person (Article 18). Third, time limits are laid down to ensure that information exchange is timely and thus effective. Finally, among the classical alternatives, it is expressly recognized that the mandatory automatic exchange of information without preconditions is the most effective means of enhancing the correct assessment of taxes in cross-border situations and fighting fraud. To this extent, Article 8 imposes the automatic exchange of available information (AEOI), from the Member State of source to the Member State of residence, regarding taxable periods as of 1 January 2014 on five initial categories of income and capital: a) income from employment; b) director's fees; c) life insurance products not covered by other Union legal instruments on exchange of information and other similar measures; d) pensions and e) ownership of and income from immovable property.

5.2. Notwithstanding that DAC entered into force on 1 January 2013 after a few months, on 12 June 2013 the European Commission released a proposal for a Council Directive amending Directive 2011/16/EU regarding mandatory AEOI in the field of taxation on dividends, capital gains, any other income generated with respect to the assets held in a financial account, and any amount with respect to which the financial institution is the creditor or the debtor, including any redemption payments and account balances (COM(2013) 348 final). Many events indeed occurred in a very short period. On 6 December 2012, the EU Commission presented an Action Plan to strengthen the fight against tax fraud and tax evasion. This Action Plan highlights the need to promote AEOI as the European and international standard of transparency and exchange of information in tax matters. On 14 May 2013, the Economic and Financial Affairs Council (ECOFIN) Council adopted conclusions welcoming the work by the Commission on developing measures to combat tax fraud, tax evasion and aggressive tax planning and recognizing the useful role the Commission Action Plan can play in this regard. On 22 May 2013, the European Council went even further, requesting the extension of AEOI at EU and global levels with a view to fighting against tax fraud, tax evasion and aggressive tax planning. On that occasion, the Commission committed itself to proposing amendments to the DAC in June 2013 to expand the scope of the AEOI in anticipation of the revision of the DAC already foreseen for 2017. Certainly, the agreements that many governments have concluded with the US regarding the US Foreign Account Tax Compliance Act (FATCA) have given further impetus to the AEOI as a way of combating tax fraud and evasion.

Because of the above political pressure, the DAC has undergone seven significant changes in just a few years, namely:

I) Directive of 9 December 2014, No. 2014/107 (DAC 2), which focuses on the integration of the EU system with the Common Reporting Standard developed by the OECD and extends the automatic exchange of information on financial accounts held by non-resident individuals, establishing a framework for such global exchange.

II) Directive of 8 December 2015, No. 2015/2376 (DAC 3), which extends the automatic exchange of information to cross-border advance tax rulings (following the Luxleaks scandal).

III) Directive of 25 May 2016, No. 2016/881 (DAC 4), which extends the mandatory automatic exchange of information among the financial administrations of Member States to the "glocally" prepared reporting by multinational enterprises concerning transfer pricing.

IV) Directive of 6 December 2016, No. 2016/2258 (DAC 5), which requires Member States to provide Tax Authorities with access to anti-money laundering information resulting from customer due diligence procedures applied by financial intermediaries in accordance with the Fourth Anti-Money Laundering Directive.

V) Directive of 25 May 2018, No. 2018/822 (DAC 6), which is one of the instruments of the so-called transparency package launched by the European Commission, following the work carried out at the OECD/G20 on the Base Erosion and Profit Shifting (BEPS) project, in line with the Final Report of Action 12 on Mandatory Disclosure Rules. It imposes an obligation on any intermediary (i.e. a person registered with a professional association providing legal, tax, or consultancy services in a Member State) who designs, markets, organizes, makes available, or manages the implementation of a cross-border arrangement in the interest of a relevant taxpayer to report it to their own Tax Administration at an early stage, that is, before it is effectively implemented.

VI) Directive of 22 March 2021, No. 2021/514 (DAC 7), which will extend, starting from 1 January 2023, the automatic reporting obligation to all digital platform operators regarding their customer sellers, whether individuals or legal entities, to the tax authorities of the Member States where they are resident.

VII) Directive of 17 October 2023, No. 10215/23 (DAC 8), which requires crypto-asset service providers to report on all transactions that involve the acquisition, disposal or exchange of cryptocurrency and other digital assets.

Finally, the European Council adopted DAC 9 on 11 March 2025 with the aim of enhancing cooperation and information exchange on minimum effective corporate taxation and facilitating the implementation of the Pillar 2 Directive. It will introduce a centralized framework for the exchange of information, allowing multinational enterprise groups to file a single top-up tax return for the entire group, thereby simplifying reporting obligations.

5.3. Administrative cooperation has thus acquired a distinct legal and solidarity dimension compared to tax harmonization, positioning itself in a complementary, if not superior, relationship with it towards the achievement of the Union's objectives, and particularly to ensure the proper functioning of the internal market. All legal prerequisites have been established to facilitate the strengthening of the operational capacities of National Tax Administrations, which are increasingly called upon to cooperate in a coordinated manner to effectively implement European law. Cooperation, without directly affecting the sensitivity of Member States in matters of non-harmonized taxes, has emerged as the most suitable choice to promote wider participation of National Administrations in the implementation of European law, in line with the principles of solidarity, subsidiarity and proportionality. All this is intended to promote a common administrative-tax culture that directly affects Tax Administrations under the increasingly strong leadership of the Commission through the TAXUD Directorate, which now formulates legislative proposals for the establishment and improvement of information exchange between Member States, monitors the implementation of legislation in Member States, and provides mechanisms and electronic interfaces to coordinate the exchange of information itself. The future is a real European Tax Agency. National Tax Administrations, despite their heterogeneity, appear to integrate on a legal-functional level, according to the forms and dynamics dictated by cooperation, operating in the interest of the Union or limited to the pursuit of common and general supranational objectives. There is no doubt that this rapid expansion of European administrative tax law, from simple assistance to bilateral cooperation, with the aim of achieving true multilateral integration, has contributed to strengthening studies and stimulating jurisprudence on the right to good administration, as written and detailed in Article 41 of the Charter of Fundamental Rights of the European Union.

In conclusion, there is an apparent contradiction between the lack of political sensitivity towards tax harmonization and the extensive administrative cooperation in tax matters that has filled the void. For the Member States, the political awareness of fighting fraud, evasion and excessive tax competition has prevailed over reluctance to work together towards a true European tax system. To put it cynically, the embarrassment of losing portions of national revenue before the eyes of public opinion has compelled Member States to overcome the discomfort of potentially losing long-term political manoeuverability over their respective tax systems, even though EU tax policy should not depend on public protests to effectively address shortcomings and progress towards common objectives.

15.6 The Collection and Exchange of Information Under Anti-Money Laundering (AML) Legislation

Everything started with the 9/11 attack to the twin towers in New York when President Bush signed into law the "Uniting and Strengthening America by Providing Appropriate Tools Required to Intercept and Obstruct Terrorism of 2001", better known as the US Patriot Act. Title III was designed as the International Money Laundering Abatement and Anti-Terrorist Financing Act of 2001, containing provisions for financial institutions for the identification of terrorists through information compliance with anyone using US jurisdictional means (as any dollar-denominated transaction could be). In theory, the Patriot Act was the perfect tool to obtain significant information on beneficial owners who were terrorists from foreign institutions, without the need to make a request for information, considering any bilateral treaty. In practice, it was the perfect tool to get as much information as possible on beneficial owners. There is clearly a link between the US Patriot Act and the "Qualified Intermediary" policy first, the FATCA strategy afterwards and the EU responses. As a perfect tsunami, this initiative expanded all over the civilized world to reaffirm the supremacy of the western world through technology, as Peter Thiel seems to encourage within his essay "The Straussian moment"; for example, in Europe, Directive (EU) 2015/849 of 20 May 2015 on the prevention of the use of the financial system for the purposes of money laundering or terrorist financing (replacing the old Directives 2005/60/EC of 26 October 2005 and 2006/70/EC of 1 August 2006) provided for stronger customer due diligence obligations on a large variety of intermediaries and professionals with the scope to intercept the "beneficial owner as the natural person(s) who ultimately owns or controls the customer and/or the natural person on whose behalf a transaction or activity is being conducted". Each single EU Member State must have a financial intelligence unit (FIU) with the power (i) to control intermediaries and professionals in their customer due diligence obligations; (ii) to collect information on the above-mentioned "beneficial owners" and (iii) to cooperate and exchange information with FIUs of other EU Member States. Since the area of the "beneficial owner" definition, or alternatively, the know-your-client (KYC) approach, under the AML is by far larger than any "beneficial owner" perimeter under tax law principles, the level of information obtained is much broader and intrusive and could lead to problems in terms of taxpayers' protection rights. It must be pointed out that there is nothing but a homogeneous approach in "beneficial owner" definitions, which could have consequences in the correct flow of information.

6.1. The latest EU anti-money laundering Directive (AMLD) is Directive (EU) 2024/1640, also known as the sixth anti-money laundering Directive (AMLD6). It was adopted on 31 May 2024 and published in the Official Journal on 19 June 2024. AMLD6 repeals the previous Directive (EU) 2015/849 (AMLD4) and introduces significant updates to strengthen the EU's AML framework: (i) Beneficial Ownership Transparency: AMLD6 mandates that Member States establish and maintain central registers of beneficial ownership for both corporate and trust structures. These registers must be accessible to competent authorities and, under certain circumstances, to the public. (ii) Enhanced Due Diligence Measures: The directive introduces stricter due diligence requirements for obliged entities, particularly concerning politically exposed persons (PEPs) and high-risk third countries. (iii) Real Estate Transparency: AMLD6 requires Member States to ensure access to information on the ownership of real estate, facilitating the identification of illicit financial flows through property transactions. (iv) Financial Intelligence Units (FIUs): The directive outlines the responsibilities and tasks of FIUs, enhancing their role in detecting and preventing money laundering and terrorist financing. (v) Supervisory Cooperation: AMLD6 emphasizes the need for effective cooperation between national supervisory authorities and competent authorities, including the establishment of supervisory colleges for cross-border coordination. AMLD6 entered into force on 9 July 2024, and Member States are required to transpose the directive into national law by 10 July 2027.

6.2. The above *tsunami wave* is clear at the international and European levels; all countries involved have anti-money laundering legislation (AML) and related organizations. It is worth noting that for all countries concerned, AML is in essence a criminal law providing limitations to the individual freedom both on the side of intermediaries and professionals as well as on the side of beneficial owners (in this latter case either for money laundering or tax-related crimes, i.e. aggressive tax avoidance, tax evasion and fraud, or, in some cases, for the so-called "self-money laundering"). AML is essentially a criminal law aiming to restore the breach of social equilibrium, and its powers of investigation need to be much more intrusive than the powers of a simple tax assessment. On the other hand, since the use of these powers may ultimately deprive individuals of their freedom within the scope of being re-educated, they should be balanced with appropriate protection rights for the same individuals whose freedom might be jeopardized when under investigation. At the present time, the European Court of Justice in the Jyske case stated that legislation that requires credit institutions to communicate information, for the purpose of combating money laundering and terrorist financing, directly to the FIU of the Member State where those institutions carry out their activities is appropriate to achieving the above-mentioned aim with no breach of Article 8 of the European Convention of Human Rights (ECHR).

6.3. One outstanding point of further investigation is the possible confusion between administrative cooperation in tax matters (less intrusive information balanced with less taxpayer protection) and judicial cooperation in tax matters (more intrusive information balanced with more taxpayer protection). The additional role of FIUs with reference to AML/KYC definitions, which are not at all homogeneous all over European Member States, may indeed contribute to this overlap, with the consequence of having an explosive cocktail of more intrusive information and less taxpayer protection.

15.7 The "Realpolitik": De-Offshoring Solutions of Equivalent Effect Other Than the Exchange of Information

The tax policy has been living all over the history of human beings, among sticks and carrots, and if AEOI, in its different perspectives, is a stick, it is now time to show what the carrots are and to expose the graduating level of fiscal sustainability from the best to the worst. In September 2010, the OECD released a comparative analysis, guidance and policy advice on offshore voluntary disclosure, where Jeffrey Owens, in the preface, stated that for years, the OECD has advocated a policy of improved international tax cooperation, including better information exchange and transparency to counter offshore tax evasion. At the same time, the OECD has been encouraging countries to examine voluntary compliance strategies to enable non-compliant taxpayers to declare income and wealth that they have in the past concealed by means of taking advantage of strict bank secrecy jurisdictions. Offshore voluntary compliance programmes offer the opportunity to maximize the benefits of improvements in transparency and exchange of information for tax purposes, to increase short-term tax revenues and to improve medium-term tax compliance. To succeed, they need to tread a fine line between encouraging non-compliant taxpayers to permanently improve their compliance (a balancing act in itself) and retaining the support and compliance of the vast majority of taxpayers who are already compliant. To do this, they need to form a part of wider voluntary compliance and enforcement strategies. They also need to be consistent with relevant rules in non-tax areas such as AML rules. On 6 December 2012, the EU Commission released the communication to the European Parliament and the Council related to an action plan to strengthen the fight against tax fraud and tax evasion where, among the guidelines to enhance tax compliance, it is suggested, on one hand, to develop common methodologies and guidelines to enhance educational measures with a view to raising taxpayers' awareness on the powers of tax administrations to obtain information from other countries, and on the other hand, to develop motivational incentives by encouraging, through common methodologies and guidelines, voluntary disclosure programmes.

7.1. There is a huge difference between voluntary disclosure and compliance. The latter is when taxpayers are motivated to comply with the tax rules since they are aware that Tax Authorities alternatively use their sovereign power to enforce their tax obligations through audits, penalties (criminal and/or administrative), interest charges and several other collection tools. On the contrary, if taxpayers do not comply with (international more than domestic) tax rules, it is probably because they are more likely to believe that tax authorities will not be able to enforce their tax obligations. This behaviour is always voluntary, but with the opposite sign. From time to time, some events break this taxpayers' assumption, although they do not automatically imply effective tax enforcement by Tax Authorities. Within this framework, the idea of voluntary disclosure may be considered: it is, in essence, an exceptional programme which allows taxpayers to disclose voluntarily undeclared income and wealth upon granting a substantial reduction of penalties (criminal and/or administrative). Of course, there is a fine line to be struck between presenting the programme as both "business as usual" and as a "special opportunity". Ideally, there should be enough perceived incentive for the targeted population to take part, without so much real incentive as to alienate the majority who are already compliant.

7.2. Whether a voluntary disclosure programme is an example of realpolitik is arguable. Much depends on the penalty reduction granted and measures to ensure sustainable compliance in the future. To a certain extent, even for the thief who gives back the stolen property, criminal law generally provides for a lower punishment on the assumption that there has been a form of redemption. There seems to be little tax morale to be addressed by legislators and governments. Many countries have adopted voluntary disclosure programmes over the years, including Belgium,

Finland, France, Germany, Spain, Sweden, the UK, the US and Italy. A step below in terms of fiscal sustainability is assigned to the tax amnesty mechanism, which occurs when a voluntary disclosure programme also grants a reduction in taxes that should have been declared. Although in most countries the taxpayer must pay the amount of tax he or she would have owed in the absence of a voluntary disclosure, some experiences of dubious fiscal sustainability are present, that is, in Belgium, Hungary and Poland.

7.3. A nature more like a tax amnesty rather than a voluntary disclosure is attributable to the so-called “Rubik” agreements, which have been proposed by Switzerland in the past years and were only concluded with Austria and the United Kingdom (negotiations with Germany and Italy have failed). In essence, it provided a withholding tax mechanism, clearing any administrative and/or criminal sanction, as a waiver of the exchange of information since Switzerland agrees to have its own financial institutions register the assets belonging to taxpayers resident in the other State, and the final withholding tax is levied at an agreed rate. Once this procedure is carried out, the tax arising from future assets of the taxpayer is collected by the Swiss FI and passed to the revenue of the other State through the Swiss Federal Tax Administration, while the client’s name and details are not disclosed. The tax privacy of the bank’s client is therefore safeguarded. On the Austrian side, a similar Rubik-style agreement has also been signed with Liechtenstein to recapture bankable assets managed by Liechtenstein trustees or fiduciaries and held by Anstalts, foundations or other similar entities. According to the Austrian Ministry of Finance, the agreement with Switzerland fulfilled the expectations about the fiscal result of the regularization of the past: in July 2013, Swiss Authorities transferred 416.7 million euros as the first tranche payment to Austria, while in September 2013, the second tranche amounted to 254.7 million euros. On the UK side, the agreement has been described as the “largest ever tax evasion settlement in UK history”, but current data appear to suggest that the estimation of £5 billion was overoptimistic. According to the Swiss scholars, Rubik agreements have the merit of combining confidentiality and compliance with different tax obligations; however, following the refusal of the German Parliament to ratify the Rubik agreement and the recent evolution of tax information exchange, especially in Europe, which indicates a significant rise of AEOI, one may wonder if Rubik agreements constitute a sustainable solution for Switzerland in the long term.

7.4. The idea of a tax solution Rubik style is not original, since the Savings Directive 2003/48/EC (abolished on 15 November 2015) already introduced something similar to the mechanism of a withholding tax on the interest payments to EU resident taxpayers instead of exchanging information from Switzerland, Liechtenstein, San Marino, Monaco and Andorra, on one side, to European countries (other than Luxembourg and Austria), on the other side, as a second-best temporary option on the way towards AEOI and the abolition of banking privilege.

7.5. On the lowest side of the fiscal sustainability scale, there are alternative sources to collect information, specifically whistleblower programmes and the acquisition of stolen bank data. It appears that several countries adopt these underground spying methods, granting a reward; that is, Austria, France, the Netherlands, Poland, Spain and the US. To a certain extent, something similar to a whistleblower programme is the duty involving financial intermediaries as well as professionals when faced with the so-called "suspicious operations" under AML. They are obliged to make a notice to the FIU, and such an obligation overrides any professional and banking secrecy.

7.6. There are several rules of law regarding the above-mentioned tax solutions, other than the exchange of information, which are crucial for any tax realpolitik measure. The fil rouge is related to the use of information, whether illegally obtained or obtained through a legal instrument which would require alternative instructions for its use. As far as the use of illegally obtained data (i.e. the LGT Bank case, the HSBC case, the UBS case, the Falciani case and, more recently the Panama Papers), it is not clear and homogeneous whether a public authority could profit from information acquired and/or received to support both an administrative tax assessment and a criminal tax investigation. In case illegally obtained data are used to support an administrative tax assessment and a criminal tax investigation, there are a number of questions involved: 1) whether the taxpayer is informed and/or allowed to be involved in the due course of inbound or outbound information procedure; 2) whether the taxpayer has the possibility to reject the request and/or the use of inbound or outbound data; and 3) whether the taxpayer can refuse to collaborate with his Tax Administration without jeopardizing his position.

7.7. The legitimacy of interference, public interest and proportionality principles applied to administrative tax assessment and criminal tax investigations may be analysed on the grounds of the ECHR sentence N.K.M. v. Hungary 14, May 2013, n. 66529/11, where it is stated that, in addition to being in accordance with the domestic law of the Contracting State, including its Constitution, the legal norms upon which the deprivation of property is based should be sufficiently accessible, precise and foreseeable in their application. As for the notion of "foreseeability", its scope depends to a considerable degree on the content of the instrument in issue, the field it is designed to cover and the number and status of those to whom it is addressed. A rule is "foreseeable" when it affords a measure of protection against arbitrary interferences by public authorities. Similarly, the applicable law must provide minimum procedural safeguards commensurate with the importance of the principle at stake (point 48 of the sentence).

7.8. The dilemma is where does the International tax policy stand between the edge of automatic exchange of information for de-offshoring and the edge of any other tax solution of equivalent effect, which may be inducing other offshoring, or, to put it another way around, where does the International tax justice stand between the Machiavellian pragmatism to challenge fundamental principles, on one hand, and the deliberative democracy, eventually in a transnational perspective, promoted by

Jurgen Habermas, on the other hand? AEOI seems to be an irreversible trend, and none of the countries involved want to give the impression of suspicion on the fairness or effectiveness of its democratic development. The OECD is pressing quite hard on the accelerator, as the accepted recommendation on CRS for automatic exchange of financial account information demonstrates: the advantage of standardization is process simplification, higher effectiveness and lower costs for all stakeholders concerned. A proliferation of different and inconsistent models would potentially impose significant costs on both government and business to collect the necessary information and operate the different models. To make it simple to understand, different interpretations of the tax residence, including double or triple residences, jeopardize AEOI (if an individual is both resident in Italy and in Switzerland and has financial assets in Switzerland, the Swiss bank shall not send financial information to Italy).

However, is it possible to declare that alternative solutions, such as voluntary disclosures, are the last resort? Is it globally true that AEOI is the best tool for democratic control over countries and their taxpayers? It is hard to find a definitive solution without being rhetorical since the history of taxation, as well as the history of the economy, is too long to be minimized with a conclusion. For example, according to the majority and minority staff report "Offshore Tax Evasion: The Effort to Collect Unpaid Taxes on Billions in Hidden Offshore Accounts" released on 26 February 2014 by the Permanent Subcommittee on Investigations at the United States Senate led by Carl Levin, FATCA's disclosure requirements have been limited and weakened by its implementing regulations and may allow many US taxpayers to continue concealing their accounts in Switzerland and elsewhere (part V, B (3) (b)(iii)). At the same time, according to the Financial Times Report "The New Switzerland?" by K. Scannell and V. Houlder, published on 9 May 2016 in South Dakota, financial assets held by local trusts increased from USD 32.8 trillion in 2006 to USD 226 trillion in 2014, and the number of trust companies increased from 20 to 86 in the same period. This is possible because the United States is strong enough to request worldwide financial information on its citizens, but it is zero generous in outbound transparency: that is, under IGA 1 concluded between Italy and the United States on 10 January 2014 at Article 2, paragraph 2, let. a), number 1), Italy is obliged to give information on "name, address, and US TIN of each Specified US Person that is an Account Holder of such account and, in the case of a Non-US Entity that, after the application of the due diligence procedures set forth in Annex I, is identified as having one or more Controlling Persons that is a Specified US Person, the name, address, and US TIN (is any) of such entity and each such Specified US Person", while in Article 2, paragraph 2, let. b), number 1), the Unites States is only obliged to give information on "name, address, and Italian TIN of any person that is a resident of Italy and is an Account Holder of the account". If Italy is going to receive this small amount of information, it is because the Florida Bankers Association and the Texas Bankers Association lost the case where they pretended not to give information at all to the IRS by claiming that IGAs would breach the *Administrative Procedure Act* and the *Regulatory Flexibility Act*, imposing on their members additional compliance costs. Hence, a company under the laws of Delaware and a trust under the laws of South Dakota, Nevada or Florida are enough for an Italian resident citizen to safely shelter financial assets from the Italian Revenue. Last but not least, H.J. Res. 41 through Public Law 115-4 of 14 February 2017 has been approved (first signature of President Trump), which nullifies the "Disclosure of Payments by Resource Extraction Issuers" rule finalized by the Securities and Exchange Commission on 17 July 2016 (the rule, mandated under the Dodd-Frank Wall Street Reform and Consumer Protection Act, requires source extraction issuers to disclose payments made to governments for the commercial development of oil, natural gas, or minerals).

If the United States, Europe and Japan, together holding 92% of the world's financial wealth of households (USD 88 trillion), decide to introduce a withholding tax on outgoing interest, dividends and royalties, following the old solution of the EU Savings Directive and the Rubik Agreements, most of the offshore appeal would be over. The same could be achieved with an internationally coordinated approach to the taxation of multinational corporations. Utopia? More likely than not. Under America First, President Trump introduced a 10% one-off tax levy on overseas earnings (standing around 1.2 trillion dollars) to encourage US companies to bring them home.

Another issue is to analyse the tension between the legitimate rights of States to protect their tax base by collecting information of taxpayers as much as possible to guarantee taxation and the legitimate rights of taxpayers to privacy and to be protected against the almighty power of these States. It seems to find more Machiavelli in Austria, Germany, Switzerland and the United States, while more Habermas is found in Belgium, the Czech Republic, Finland, France, Italy, Poland, Portugal and Sweden, and in between are Luxembourg, the Netherlands, Russia, Spain and the UK. If future development can be drawn, this has to do with the need for a sustainable balance between AEOI and the taxpayer's right to ask for protection before any technological intrusion in their personal sphere.

Two concluding remarks on de-offshoring. The first is related to the relation between unilateralism and cooperation, since the latter means sharing the revenue related to "datafication" with other members of the International Community, while any unilateral initiative brings money straight to the domestic revenue. As the novel "The Leopard" by Giuseppe Tomasi di Lampedusa warns, everything must change because everything remains as it is, and the feeling is that this ocean of information, cooperation and recommendation risks being useless in the long run or, better, could only be useful for large but not all taxpayers. The second has to do with the other face of transparency and privacy. In principle, the United States and Europe have different views on what privacy means. While in the United States, privacy is meant as the right of a consumer to know how and where their personal data is being held and must be balanced with the interests of the business sector and society; in Europe, privacy is prominently a matter of the dignity of the human being, hence a fundamental right of citizens within the society. So far, automatic exchange of tax information is an example of the growing State control on "datafication", like a fuel for impenetrable State authoritarianism. The need for future investigation is more perceived on the individual as taxpayer rather than on the individual as consumer. The mission in this future scenario is probably to analyse how far supranational rules governing big data are being democratically developed, with the scope to go beyond the proportionality principle and tailor some sustainable protection rules for the taxpayer.

15.8 Trusts, Foundations and the Like

Many times, in the booklet, the words 'trust' and 'foundations' have been used together with 'corporate vehicles' to indicate solutions to create a diaphragm between wealth and income, on one side, and related owners, hopefully taxpayers, on the other side.

Back in the twelfth century, the English knights, before leaving to go and fight in the Holy Land, without having the certainty of returning home, transferred their properties and wealth to a trustee according to the rules of common law (close to Roman law); the conflicts that arose between the wives and heirs of the knight (dead) and the trustee full owner, irresolvable following the common law, were regulated according to equity by the Chancellor, holder of the King's conscience. Hence, trust is an institution of ancient lineage that synthesizes the experience of common law (in the relationship between the settlor and the trustee) and equity law (between the trustee and the beneficiaries) on which English law is based.

Therefore, it is embodied in a triangular legal relationship based on the trust that the settlor places in the trustee to whom he transfers, by deed *inter vivos* or *mortis causa*, his assets and rights so that the trustee (who over the centuries has transformed himself from a priest to a banker, to the point of assuming the professional guise of a trust company) can administer them, with the rights and powers of a real owner, in the interest of one or more beneficiaries (relatives) of the settlor or for a pre-established purpose. The mobility of beneficiaries (think about the Grand Tours in the Enlightenment period) and the related circulation of trust fund assets made trust relationships touch, over the centuries, jurisdictions other than the UK.

Its notable international diffusion in civil law jurisdictions has been particularly favoured by the Convention on the Law of Trusts and their Recognition, signed in The Hague on 1 July 1985 and entered into force on 1 January 1992, which gave rise to a series of new rules, such as determining a sort of international model. In addition to the Anglo-Saxon tax havens that already provided for it, those of Roman legal culture have also been added (the most striking case is that of Liechtenstein), generally providing for a favourable tax regime for the trust, subject to requirements, to attract investments that can be made through this legal instrument.

It is often required that the settlor and beneficiaries are non-residents of the tax haven and that the trust fund does not include assets located in the territory of the tax haven. It is also often required, although sometimes not for purely tax purposes, that the trust deed be registered in the local public registers.

In many offshore jurisdictions, if the requirements are met, trusts may benefit from a total exemption from any form of taxation, be it on income, assets, or inheritances and gifts. Usually, therefore, the only form of tax is that levied upon registration, while, at the same time, income taxes as well as inheritance and gift taxes can be avoided in the rest of the world.

The fundamental element for trust to be legitimate from a tax point of view is that the trustee must really, and not fictitiously, interpose himself between the assets and rights that have been attributed to him and the settlor, on the one hand, and the beneficiaries, on the other hand.

In order for the interposition to be real and not fictitious, the trust must be irrevocable (i.e. the settlor can no longer claim back the ownership of the assets he has transferred to the trustee) and discretionary (i.e. the beneficiaries must not have the right to claim the payment of the income that is produced on the trust fund, and the trustee must have the discretionary power to decide whether and to what extent to benefit them).

The main dialogue with Revenue is, from the perspective of the settlor, to demonstrate that he has left the scene and does not significantly influence the decisions of the trustee (for example, through the assumption of a protector role which should generally be reserved for a person in the settlor's Family or close to the settlor's Family); from the perspective of the beneficiaries, however, it is essential to assess that the beneficiaries do not have the availability of the trust fund, which is often not true.

In short, since the application of taxes in the majority of the most advanced States is subject to the circumstance that one has substantial availability of the source (asset or right) of the income, the settlor and beneficiaries must be convinced that the only one who has availability (even if conditional) of the income and the assets that produce it is the trustee.

The concept of beneficiary deserves clarification: it should not coincide with that of the beneficial owner, an expression used in the banking and financial world, which complies with anti-money laundering legislation to identify the person from whom the funds originate, typically the settlor. Even if the current trend in international and comparative tax law is precisely that of overlapping the notion of beneficiary with the much more invasive AML notion of "ultimate beneficial owner" (UBO).

The discussion, therefore, focuses on the analysis of the management powers that the trustee has in concrete terms. If he has broad, effective and discretionary powers of administration, such that he can decide how to dispose of the sources of income and the income elements, then the trust will be a real interposition, and the beneficiary will not have tax obligations in the State of residence. This is despite the awareness that, from a strictly economic point of view, the trustee cannot enrich himself with the income of the trust, having to remit these (sooner or later) to the beneficiaries or to a purpose.

Naturally, the determination of powers should not be based only on the trust deed and the governing law, but every other element useful for determining the effective powers should also be examined. It would, in fact, be too simple to base the validity of a trust only on what emerges from the documents, leaving ample margins for abusive or simulated uses, even though it may be particularly difficult to ascertain which powers the trustee exercises in administering the trust.

More so, since any (undue) influence on the trustee's activity, which limits his powers, may not be evident from documentary evidence. It is true that, from this perspective, it may be useful to analyse any letters of wishes which, if used improperly, may become a tool to limit the trustee's powers in practice. But even more important is the analysis of the actual nature of the relationship between trustee and settlor and between these and the possible protector.

In fact, to determine which powers the trustee exercises, it is necessary to verify whether there are subjects who constantly direct their attention, even informally. However, it should be noted that the limitations of the trustee's powers can determine the inviolability of the trust, where the essence of the entrustment to the trustee is annulled. This occurs when, from an activity of mere management control, one passes on to actions aimed at directing the trustee's activity.

8.1. Unlike trusts, foundations, typically those under Liechtenstein law, are entities with a legal personality to which the founder transfers assets as an endowment for the pursuit of a specific purpose. Naturally, the founder is represented at the incorporation, with a minimum of thirty thousand Swiss francs, by a trust company; this solution guarantees the most absolute confidentiality, a characteristic for which this legal instrument has been appreciated throughout the world, as emerged in the investigation conducted by the American Senate against the LGT group of Vaduz.

The foundation is typically established for the interests of a family, and its function is to increase, manage, and hold an estate for the maintenance of the members of the founder's family or people close to him, who are defined as beneficiaries. The management and representation of the foundation towards third parties is ensured by the foundation board, which acts as its representative, of which at least one board member must be resident in the Principality and have the relevant government qualification as an accountant or lawyer. The relationships between the founder and the foundation board, and those between the foundation board and the beneficiaries, are perfected in the foundation regulations, which are not required to be registered in the public register and therefore guarantee the absolute confidentiality of the subjects involved.

8.2. Remaining in the Principality of Liechtenstein, there is another legal vehicle often used for tax reasons, and that is the Anstalt.

An Anstalt is a distinctive legal structure between a foundation and a corporation, blending the features of both. While it has the independent legal personality and operational flexibility of a company, it also shares the private, family oriented nature of a foundation.

An Anstalt is usually formed by a founder who sets it up for a specific purpose, often for managing assets, holding investments, or passing on wealth to future generations. Unlike traditional companies, they typically do not issue shares. Instead, control is exercised through a board of directors or a similar governing body, and its purpose may benefit specific individuals or be used for broader wealth management goals.

Because of its confidential structure, an Anstalt has long been a favoured vehicle for individuals and families seeking to protect their assets, maintain privacy, and create flexible inheritance arrangements.

Liechtenstein has a flat corporate income tax rate of 12.5%, which applies to an Anstalt as well. This is relatively low compared to many other jurisdictions. In practice, most Anstalts, especially those with passive income, pay a minimum tax of around CHF 1800 per year, making them cost-effective to maintain. Liechtenstein does not impose withholding taxes on dividends, interest, or royalties that are paid out by the Anstalt. This simplifies international transactions and distribution to beneficiaries.

Beyond taxes, Anstalt is also valued for its discretion. While global regulations such as the common reporting standard (CRS) and anti-money laundering (AML) laws have introduced transparency obligations, Liechtenstein remains a jurisdiction with a strong legal tradition of protecting private ownership. The internal structure and beneficiaries of an Anstalt are not publicly disclosed, although they are known to the Financial Authorities.

8.3. Beyond foundations and Anstalt, the Principality of Liechtenstein also includes regular corporations subject to a flat corporate income tax rate of 12.5%, which was introduced only under the new Tax Act ("Steuergesetz") of 2011.

There was no corporate taxation at the time when Diego Armando Maradona used to play with *Società Sportiva Calcio Napoli* during the years 1984–1991. *El Pibe de Oro* was a tax resident in Italy and, in agreement with the Club, interposed a corporation in Vaduz to manage the rights of his image so that anytime he was playing his wonderful football in the Naples San Paolo Stadium, the Club used to pay to the corporation royalties by far much bigger than the compensation he used to get as a football player. *La Mano de Dios* was neither paying income taxes on the above payments, nor was the Club applying withholding taxes on social security contributions. A perfect dribbling for more than four million euros tax-free (around eight billion liras at the time).

The Tax Police of Naples claimed that the triangular scheme based in Vaduz was a fictitious interposition between Maradona and the Club to evade income tax. The case went to the Tax Court when Maradona had already left Naples (Tax Court decision 20 December 1993, n. 3230, in favour of the Tax Administration, and Tax Court of Appeal decision 6 September 1994, n. 126, in favour of Maradona and the Club), but it never landed in the Supreme Court since a tax amnesty cleared the dispute and the match ended in a draw. Very much the Italian style of the time.

Maradona was a champion also in dribbling the Italian Revenue (the Naples Stadium is today the Maradona Stadium), but many other football players (e.g. the Argentinian Lionel Messi, the Portuguese Cristiano Ronaldo, the Brazilian Neymar Jr., and the Spanish Xabi Alonso) have used the same triangular scheme with more or less success in minimizing tax liabilities.

15.9 The Beneficial Owner: Too Many Times, a Missing Taxpayer

A fundamental aspect of modern tax transparency and the exchange of information mechanisms is the concept of beneficial ownership. This term refers to the true economic owner of an asset, income, or financial instrument, as opposed to the legal owner, who may hold the title on paper but does not derive the actual benefits. Taxes are based on substance more than on form, and this is the reason why the economic owner is preferable to the legal owner, who, in many triangular cases, hides the first.

The concept of beneficial ownership has been developed in international tax law primarily through many sources: (i) Articles 1 and 10–12 of the OECD Model Tax Convention, which restrict treaty benefits to taxpayers who are the actual beneficial owners of income; (ii) financial action task force (FATF) Recommendations, which require countries to maintain accurate and updated beneficial ownership information to prevent tax evasion, money laundering and terrorist financing; (iii) EU Directives (AML and DAC), which mandate EU Member States to maintain central registers of beneficial owners.

The identification of a beneficial owner is crucial for preventing treaty shopping and abusive tax arrangements. Many multinational corporations and high-net-worth individuals structure their holdings through multiple layers of entities in different jurisdictions, obscuring true ownership. This is the reason why there are key initiatives to counter an international reaction: (i) Country-by-Country Reporting (CbCR) under BEPS Action 13; (ii) Automatic Exchange of Beneficial Ownership Information under CRS and FATCA and (iii) Mandatory Disclosure Rules (MDRs) require professionals to report aggressive tax planning schemes.

Despite advancements in regulation, several challenges persist, such as the use of nominee shareholders and directors by offshore jurisdictions that often allow nominee services, making it difficult to determine the true owner and complex corporate structures, or multilayered structures involving trusts, foundations and shell companies to disguise ownership. Finally, while CRS and FATCA have improved transparency, discrepancies remain between jurisdictions.

The trend towards greater tax transparency continues, with public beneficial ownership registers and enhanced reporting obligations likely to be the next steps. The ongoing efforts of the OECD, EU and FATF suggest that global standards will further tighten, reducing the avenues for tax evasion and aggressive tax planning.

The "beneficial ownership" clause is recognized by the international community as one of the tools to counter certain forms of "treaty shopping", namely that specific form of abuse of international treaties implemented through the establishment of conduit companies, which are interposed between the State of the source and the State of the final beneficiary of the income.

The goal of such an avoidance strategy is to provide types of income flows (*i.e.* dividends, interest or royalties) by eliminating or reducing the withholding tax through the exploitation of the benefits provided by international agreements against double taxation on income or EU Directives.

In this regard, Articles 10, 11 and 12 of the OECD Model contain the anti-abuse clause (referred to as 'beneficial owner' or 'beneficial ownership'), which allows for the disapplication, from an anti-avoidance perspective, of the most favourable conditions provided by EU Directives or bilateral agreements between various countries in the world.

Moreover, the beneficial ownership clause also helps to resolve coordination issues arising from the absence, in tax treaties, of clauses such as the "subject to tax" clause (which requires the residence State—having been granted exclusive taxing rights over a specific item of income—to effectively exercise such taxing rights) or the "switch-over" clause (which allows the residence State, having committed to exempt a certain type of income in favour of exclusive taxation in the source State, to replace the exemption method with the credit method for foreign taxes in all cases where the source State has either not taxed the income or has done so only nominally).

15.10 The Beneficial Owner of the OECD Model

The term 'beneficial owner' was formally introduced into the international legal framework through its explicit inclusion in the 1977 OECD Model Tax Convention, which serves as a guiding instrument for States in the negotiation and drafting of bilateral tax treaties currently in force.

At first, the status of the beneficial owner was only delineated negatively, and its recognition was not subject to a specific economic/substantial assessment.

Then, the concept of a beneficial owner has progressively developed, and since the 2003 OECD Model, substantive profiles have been increasingly emphasized.

Such an approach was recently transfused into the Commentary to the 2014 OECD Model, which highlights the effective powers of the recipient to dispose of and enjoy income and the requirement of tax liability that is not merely abstract. The additions to the Commentary on Articles 10, 11 and 12 have thus made it possible to better circumscribe the notion of beneficial owner.

According to the current wording of the Commentary on Articles 10, 11 and 12 of the OECD Model, it can be stated that (i) the concept of beneficial owner is to be interpreted as a concept of international tax law and not by reference to a possible notion derivable from domestic law; (ii) the status of beneficial owner is closely linked to the presence of discretionary power (in the sense of power of legal and economic disposal) on the part of the recipient of the income; (iii) the presence of discretionary power is allowed even in the presence of a retransfer obligation, provided that this obligation is not subordinate and causally connected to the receipt of a specific income; (iv) the assessment of beneficial owner status is to be understood from the point of view of economic substance, *that is,* by verifying, firstly, the presence of an economic benefit for the recipient and, secondly, the proportionality of that benefit in relation to the duties performed and risks assumed.

It is worth pointing out that the beneficial ownership clause, although applicable to interest, royalties and dividends alike, tends to assume a more nuanced connotation when applied to the latter category of income, reflecting its specific characteristics. As opposed to interest and royalties, dividends are transferred along the corporate chain based on associative contracts rather than synallagmatic agreements. This means that when it comes to dividends, a repayment obligation can exist only if the recipient is an agent, nominee, or conduit company acting as a fiduciary or administrator.

In addition, it is not necessary for the recipient to have full and unconditional rights of use and enjoyment over the dividend if there is no obligation to pass it on to another person.

15.11 The Beneficial Owner of the EU Tax Law

As previously stated, Articles 10, 11 and 12 of the OECD Model deal with the taxation of interest, dividends or royalties and provide for a limitation on the rate of tax which may be imposed by the source State, but only if such interest, dividends or royalties are beneficially owned by a resident of the other contracting State. These three types of income are also addressed by secondary EU legislation, *that is,* the Interest and Royalty Directive 2003/49/C (IRD) for cross-border interest and royalty payments between associated companies and the Parent-Subsidiary Directive 2011/96/EU (PSD) for cross-border inter-company dividends. Both Directives provide for a complete abolition of source taxation, but only the Interest and Royalties Directive explicitly addresses the question of beneficial ownership. The scope is to avoid extra-EU investors and corporations using EU special purpose vehicles (notably in the Netherlands, Luxembourg and Denmark) to channel their investments in other EU Member States.

IRD uses the concept of beneficial ownership in several provisions, and only those receiving payments, who are the beneficial owners of the payment, may enjoy the benefits of tax harmonization; those who cannot be viewed as such will be denied the withholding tax exemption based on the IRD. This understanding confirms that the provision has an anti-abuse purpose, since its main objective is to deny the harmonized regime to persons (individuals or corporations) who are not receiving payments for their benefit. The beneficial owner status is, therefore, a requisite to enjoy the IRD benefits.

IRD requires the State in which the company making the payments is resident (and which deducts such payments from its taxable income) to waive any taxing rights over group companies resident in other Member States or permanent establishments of non-EU companies located in a Member State. Such an exemption regime applies when (i) the recipient qualifies as a company *liable to tax* and (ii) the recipient is the real beneficiary of the payments, *that is, subject to tax* on such income items in the Member State of residence or establishment.

PSD concerns the common system of taxation applicable to parent companies and their subsidiaries established in different Member States and aims to eliminate both economic double taxation arising from cross-border profit distributions within corporate groups and double non-taxation, which may result from the exemption granted in the Member State of the parent company.

To this end, PSD provides for a withholding tax exemption in the source State (*i.e.* the State of the subsidiary), subject to certain conditions, as well as an obligation for the Member State of the parent company to either exempt the income from taxation or grant credit for the underlying tax, thereby offsetting the taxes paid at the level of the subsidiary. This results in a mitigation of the two levels of taxation borne by the parent company in connection with the distribution of profits: the withholding tax applied in the State of the subsidiary and the corporate income tax payable by the parent company, in its State of residence, on the profits so received.

Hence, the abolition of withholding tax in the State of the subsidiary could result in the elimination of juridical double taxation as an indirect effect of the Directive.

This aspect clarifies why, as previously mentioned, PSD differs from IRD in the absence of any express reference to the notion of beneficial ownership, both in the original text and in its current version. As a matter of fact, since PSD aims to eliminate both juridical and economic double taxation by requiring coordination between the Member States of the parent and the subsidiary, explicitly identifying the dividend recipient as the beneficial owner appears to be of limited relevance.

The Beneficial Ownership According to the European Court of Justice of the European Union (ECJ): The Danish Cases

In 2019, the Court of Justice of the European Union (ECJ) delivered its judgements in a series of landmark cases concerning the Danish withholding tax regime applicable to dividends and interest paid by Danish companies to entities established in other Member States. Substantively, the Danish Cases involved the interpretation of both IRD (Joined Cases C-115/16, C-118/16, and C-299/16) and PSD (Joined Cases C-116/16 and C-117/16).

Regarding PSD, the ECJ affirmed that even in the absence of a specific anti-abuse provision under domestic or treaty law, National Courts and Tax Authorities can still deny the benefits of a Directive in cases of fraud or abuse. (Joined Cases C-116/16 and C-117/16, paragraph 75). In other words, when assessing entitlement to the benefits of the Parent-Subsidiary Directive, it is not necessary to invoke the beneficial ownership clause, as developed in tax treaties or in the IRD. The general prohibition of abuse is a self-standing and inherent principle of EU law.

Turning to the beneficial ownership requirement under the IRD, the Court clarified that the notion of a beneficial owner must be given an autonomous meaning under EU law. It cannot be defined with reference to potentially divergent concepts found in domestic laws. According to the ECJ, such a concept is rooted in economic reality and designates an entity that genuinely enjoys the income received.

Indeed, a company resident in a Member State may be considered the beneficial owner of interest or royalties only if it receives such income for its own benefit and not as an intermediary, representative, authorized signatory, or fiduciary acting on behalf of another entity. In such a case, the company must have the freedom to decide the use and destination of the funds received.

Accordingly, the ECJ endorsed a *look-through* approach, whereby Tax Authorities may investigate whether, beyond an interposed company (even if lacking beneficial ownership status), lies an EU-resident entity that qualifies as the genuine recipient of the income and thus may be entitled to benefit from the exemption under the relevant Directive or convention. Importantly, the mere existence of a conduit entity does not, in and of itself, constitute an abusive arrangement. The decisive factor is the economic substance and function of the underlying structure.

In practical terms, when the application of the IRD is contested, Tax Authorities are required to follow a structured procedural approach: (i) they must assess whether the direct recipient of the income qualifies as the beneficial owner; (ii) if not, a look-through analysis must be conducted to identify any underlying EU-resident entity that may hold such status; (iii) if no such entity exists, the exemption under the Directive cannot be granted and (iv) in any case, the absence of beneficial ownership is a significant indicator that may justify further investigation into the existence of an abusive arrangement.

Finally, as to the allocation of the burden of proof, it falls on the taxpayer to demonstrate that the objective conditions for the application of IRD are met. Conversely, where Tax Authorities intend to deny the benefits of IRD on grounds of abuse, they bear the burden of proving the constituent elements of the abusive practice, considering all relevant indicators, including the fact that the recipient of the income is not its beneficial owner.

15.12 The Beneficial Owner of the Italian Tax Law

Under Italian law, the tax treatment of outbound payments of dividends, interest and royalties to companies established in other EU Member States reflects the implementation of key EU Directives intended to foster cross-border investment and eliminate juridical and economic double taxation within the internal market. Specifically, PSD and IRD have been transposed into domestic legislation by means of Articles 26-*quater* and 27-*bis* of Presidential Decree no. 600 of 29 September 1973, the Assessment Tax Code (ATC), and are complemented by the rules set out in Article 89 of the Italian Income Tax Code (ITC) for inbound dividends.

As regards dividends, Italian tax legislation provides for a full exemption from withholding tax where the distribution is made by an Italian-resident subsidiary to a parent company established in another EU Member State. Such exemption, governed by Article 27-*bis*, applies provided that the recipient company (i) directly holds at least 10% of the share capital of the distributing entity; (ii) holds participation for an uninterrupted period of at least one year; (iii) adopts one of the legal forms mentioned in the Annex to the Directive; and (iv) is subject, in its State of residence, to corporate income tax without the possibility of opting for a tax exemption.

When the above conditions are met, the exemption may be applied at the source, provided that the beneficiary submits appropriate documentation to the withholding agent, including a certificate of residence and a declaration of compliance with the statutory requirements. If the exemption is not applied at the time of payment, the foreign shareholder may apply for a refund in accordance with the procedure set out in Article 26-*quater*, if the substantive conditions are met.

Turning to interest and royalties, the exemption from withholding the tax provided for in Article 26-*quater* transposes the provisions of the IRD. The rule applies to payments made by an Italian-resident company to an associated company resident in another EU Member State or to a permanent establishment of such a company located in another Member State. The exemption is subject to structural conditions, namely, the existence of a corporate link: one company must hold, directly or indirectly, at least 25% of the capital or voting rights of the other, or both must be directly held by a third company meeting the same ownership threshold. The shareholding must be maintained for a minimum period of two years.

In addition to the ownership requirement, the exemption applies only if the recipient qualifies as the beneficial owner of the income and is effectively liable to corporate taxation in its State of residence. As with dividends, the exemption must be supported by formal documentation, including a residence certificate and a declaration confirming that substantive and legal conditions have been satisfied. In the absence of such documentation, an Italian withholding tax, generally levied at a rate of 26%, was applied.

Outside the scope of EU harmonization, tax relief may be available under bilateral tax treaties concluded by Italy. In these situations, pursuant to Article 27, paragraph 3, D.P.R. 600/1973, the foreign recipient may apply for the reduced rates or exemptions set out in the relevant tax treaty, provided they can demonstrate that the necessary conditions, including tax residence and beneficial ownership, are satisfied.

Italian Case Law on Beneficial Owner of Dividends

As outlined in paragraph 5 of this opinion, Article 27-*bis* of ATC, in accordance with the PSD transposed, does not explicitly include a beneficial ownership clause for outbound dividend payments. Nevertheless, Italian case law has progressively clarified that the beneficial ownership clause is applicable to dividends, as it is to interests and royalties.

Furthermore, the Italian Supreme Court has held that Article 10-*bis* of Law no. 212/2000 on anti-abuse in tax law is the only legal basis that may be relied upon to deny the dividend exemption regime in favour of EU subsidiary companies, even when the conditions laid down in Article 27-*bis* are met.

Given this premise, the main conclusions of Italian case law on the beneficial ownership clause are set forth below. The Italian Supreme Court, with leading decision no. 6005/2023, established a decisive principle regarding the evidentiary burden borne by those asserting beneficial ownership for tax purposes. The determination of the beneficial owner involves three autonomous tests: (i) the *substantive business activity test*; (ii) the *dominion test* and (iii) the *business purpose test*.

More specifically, the *substantive business activity test* is intended to verify whether the entity receiving the dividend income conducts a genuine economic activity, characterized by an effective presence in the State of Source (i.e. it is engaged in real business activities, and it has offices and operational facilities). Once it has been demonstrated that the company is not an artificial structure, the next step is to satisfy the second test. The *dominion test* is intended to check whether the entity can freely dispose of the income received or whether it has an obligation to pass it on to a third person (the so-called *back-to-back arrangement*). The obligation to pass on the income received to a third person may arise from a contract or be inferred from factual elements, such as, for example, (i) the brief period between the receipt of interest and the payment of the loan instalment; (ii) the regularity of transfers to the parent company; (iii) the low profit margin on the received interest; (iv) the identity of the management between the foreign intermediary company and the final recipient of the income flow and (v) the fact that the foreign intermediary company neither approves the financing nor bears the risk, nor can waive the amounts loaned.

When a company fails to demonstrate that it meets the dominion test criteria, it cannot be regarded as a beneficial owner. Nevertheless, this does not prevent it from enjoying other rights and freedoms granted under the Treaty on the Functioning of the European Union.

Once the substantive business activity and dominion tests have been satisfied, the remaining requirement to meet is the business purpose test. The *business purpose test* aims to evaluate the reasons behind the entity's involvement in the cross-border dividend flow, particularly whether it serves a legitimate business purpose or functions as a conduit company to exploit an undue favourable tax treatment.

The Italian Supreme Court has also examined the allocation of the burden of proof between the Tax Authority and the taxpayer, stating that the company seeking to benefit from the tax regime designed to avoid double taxation and to allocate taxing rights between different States is required to provide evidence of meeting a series of conditions and of successfully passing the above-mentioned three tests.

Lastly, it should be remembered that the Italian Supreme Court, in decision no. 6050/2023 and recently by decision no. 4427/2025, adopting the position of the ECJ, specified that if the third company for which the conduit company acts fulfils the requirements to benefit from the exemption regime of the Convention or the Directive, the tax benefit must be recognized (the so-called look-through approach). The rationale of the look-through approach is to investigate if the beneficial owner would have been theoretically entitled to benefit from a given regime or if it attempted to obtain it by exploiting a third interposed party. In a nutshell, if the "interposer" is entitled to benefit from the exemptions provided for by the Directives, the "interposition" of another company cannot be regarded as tax-driven.

References

Avi-Yonah RS, Mazzoni G (2016) Taxation and human rights: a delicate balance. In: Michigan Law, Public Law and Legal Theory Research Paper, Series Paper n. 520

Birkenfeld BC (2016) The Lucifer's Banker. Greenleaf Book Group Llc

Brabazon M (2019) International taxation of trust income: principles, planning and design. Cambridge University Press

Brittain-Catlin W (2005), Offshore, the dark side of the global economy, Farrar, Straus and Giroux, New York.

Cobham A, Garcia-Bernardo J (2020) Time for the EU to close its own tax havens. Tax Justice Network

Dietsch P (2015) Catching capital: the ethics of tax competition. Oxford University Press

Geringer S (2022) The EU's uncoordinated approach to tax avoidance and tax abuse in relation to "uncooperative" tax jurisdictions. Intertax 50(3)

Hamra C, Korving JJAM (2021) Beneficial ownership interpreted, to what extent are the OECD and the EU on the same wavelength? Intertax 49(3)

Marino G (2017) International and European measures for de-offshoring: global ambitions and local hypocrisies. Intertax 45(8/9)

OECD (1998) Harmful tax competition: an emerging global issue. Paris

OECD (2018) Automatic Exchange of Information: Implementation Report 2018. Paris

Palan R, Murphy R, Chavagneux C (2010) Tax havens: how globalization really works. Cornell University Press

Saint-Amans P (2023) Paradis fiscaux, comment on a changé le cours de l'histoire, Editions du Seuil.

Thiel P (2007) The Straussian moment.

Vlcek W (2017) Offshore finance and global governance: disciplining the tax nomad. Palgrave Macmillan

Zucman G (2015) The hidden wealth of nations: the scourge of tax havens. University of Chicago Press

The manufacturer's authorised representative in the EU is Springer Nature Customer Service Centre GmbH, Europaplatz 3, 69115 Heidelberg, Germany. If you have any concerns regarding our products, please contact ProductSafety@springernature.com

Printed and bound by CPI Group (UK) Ltd, Croydon, CR0 4YY
16/09/2026
02217795-0001